ESSENTIAL
Bowling

ESSENTIAL
Bowling

**MICHAEL
BENSON**

The Lyons Press

FIRST EDITION

Designed by PageMasters & Company

Printed in Canada
10 9 8 7 6 5 4 3 2 1

Library of Congress Cataloging-in-Publication Data
Benson, Michael
 Essential bowling / Michael Benson.
  p. cm.
 Includes index.
 ISBN 1–55821–968–4
 1. Bowling I. Title.
 GV903.B46 2000
 794.7—dc21   99–42539
                                CIP

To Trina Treu

CONTENTS

ACKNOWLEDGMENTS

The author wishes to thank the following individuals and organizations, without whose help the writing of this book would have been, well, a heck of a lot harder: Lisa, Matthew, and Tekla Benson, Jake Elwell, Anthony J. Grasso, Phil Hamric, John Illiano, Becky Koh, Rita Lascaro, Mark Lanes (Brooklyn, New York), George Napolitano, Greig O'Brien, MaryLouise O'Neill, the Professional Bowlers Association, Kathleen D. Schlaffer, Milburn Smith, Bert Randolph Sugar, Rachel Thomas, Timber Lanes (Abington, Massachusetts), Colin Touhey, and Ruthcarol Touhey.

INTRODUCTION
The Twenty-First Century Bowler

THERE WAS A TIME, back in the 1950s and '60s, when America's best bowlers were among our country's most famous athletes. Just as many people knew Don Carter and Dick Weber as knew Willie Mays and Mickey Mantle of baseball fame. Bowling was on TV two or three times a week, and brand-new shiny bowling centers were opening along every suburban highway.

But that was forty years ago. After peaking in the mid-1960s, interest in bowling slowly began to subside. In the 1980s, those same bowling centers along the suburban highways, no longer quite so shiny, were being converted into supermarkets and workout centers and the like. By the 1990s, the stars of the Pro Bowlers Tour were no longer household names. Nothing against pro bowlers, but it is safe to say that Mark McGwire is a lot more famous in the United States than Ray Williams, Jr.

Ah, but what goes around comes around, and all indications are that bowling's popularity is once again on the upswing. Indeed, bowling is at the dawn of a new golden age. With hot new superstars and a new weekly TV show on CBS, I predict that millions of Americans who previously had no interest in the sport will soon become bowlers and bowling fans.

The most promising and popular of today's superstars is five-foot-seven, 240-pound Rudy Kasimakis of Gouldsboro, Pennsylvania, who has come to the Pro Bowlers Tour by way of the nocturnal world of action bowling—that's "action" as in *gambling*. (And if you think bowlers don't gamble, then you'll believe that Minnesota Fats was an altar boy.)

Like billiards, bowling is a sport that's intrinsically connected with a saloon atmosphere. For many years bowling was a smoking-and-drinking sport. Action bowling in particular conjures up dark images of an alley at 3 A.M., closed except for the bar and two lanes where the "action" is taking place. Bowlers bet on themselves, and spectators bet on the bowler of their choice in what are usually one-on-one challenge matches—often the house pro versus an unknown.

The thirty-four-year-old Kasimakis grew up in Long Island, New York, but now lives in Pennsylvania, in the Poconos. He's famous for his charisma, talent, and courage: a combination of qualities that is perhaps unprecedented in the sport. He's been called "the Tasmanian Devil of bowling," a man who attacks every game as if it were a matter of life and death—and, who knows, there might have been a few games that were.

Kasimakis joined the PBA (Professional Bowlers Association) Tour—where he competes against Walter Ray Williams, Jr., Dale Eagle, Chris Barnes, Steve Jaros, and the rest of the greatest bowlers in the world—after twelve years of being on the road, traveling from alley to alley, from Deer Park, Long Island, to deep in the heart of Texas, sometimes entering broke and leaving with fists, pockets, and a bowling bag stuffed with cash.

He'd play games called Four-Game Freeze-Out, in which the first bowler to be ahead by four games won the entire pot, no matter how long it took. He was known to bet extraordinary amounts of money on a single frame. Every once in a while, to make things more interesting, he would spot his opponent an advantage—by agreeing to deliver the ball from behind the scorer's table, for example. On some nights the games would become even more bizarre, such as the time he bowled a lowest-score-wins match, with the stipulation that at least one pin had to be knocked down with each ball.

Kasimakis is reluctant to give details, because he doesn't want his wife, Nancy, to know the specifics.

"I never knew what went on at those things," she says.

And, since he always seemed to come home with more money than he left with, she didn't ask too many questions.

Today, Kasimakis is a balding bulldog with a black goatee. His nickname is Rudy Revs because he throws every ball at twenty-four miles per hour, with precisely twenty-four revolutions of the ball from release to contact with the pins. That combination of velocity and tight spin makes the lane rumble and causes a frighteningly violent reaction when ball meets pins. Watching Revs get tapped is more exciting than seeing most bowlers get a strike.

Kasimakis's delivery is unbelievable, with its seemingly exaggerated backswing and wrist cock. According to Nancy, who's also an excellent bowler, his real talent is as a ball driller. She says he knows more about how to drill the holes in a bowling ball than any other man alive.

Stories spread about his late-night challenges and victories. Not long after he joined the pro tour, people started coming from miles around to watch him bowl, to see if he was half the guy folks said he was. Nobody was disappointed. In February 1999, 4,000 fans showed up at the Flagship Open in Erie, Pennsylvania. Their cheers were deafening while Kasimakis was just warming up. Like fans attending pro-wrestling matches, his followers brought along signs that said things like SHOW ME THE RUDY and RUDY 3:16.

Some have called Rudy the Dennis Rodman of bowling. (Which, if there is any truth in it at all, has nothing to do with hairstyles. Kasimakis's hair is more in the tradition of 1960s bowler Ray Bluth than Rodman—shinier from the light off his scalp than from hair

With hot new stars like Rudy Kasimakis thrilling crowds, bowling is anticipating a boom in popularity.

dye.) With Rudy in the house, bowling fans can be assured of one thing: They're going to get "a hell of a show," as Kasimakis puts it.

Both CBS and the PBA are dedicated to giving bowling a stylish new image, including arena seating, gold pins, blaring rock and roll, and highly partisan crowds. Kasimakis would appear to be the odds-on favorite to become bowling's first TV star of the twenty-first century. Rudy Kasimakis will take that bet.

Although there's something in this book for everyone, *Essential Bowling* was designed for you newcomers, those of you who are discovering the excitement of bowling for the first time. If you've been a bowling fan for the past thirty years, bowl in three leagues and have five bowling balls, you'll find that you already know most of the information in this book. (But read those sections anyway. Sometimes I sprinkle in jokes.) However, even veterans of the lanes can learn something about the history of bowling or about the offshoots of such standard tenpin bowling as duckpins, candlepins, and Canadian fivepin.

But, for those of you who are relatively new to the sport, this book is crammed with information that you're going to find useful. So the next time someone comes up to you and complains that a high hit just caused the Double Pinochle, you'll know precisely what they're talking about.

Read on, and the answers will be yours.

CHAPTER 1
Entering the Alley

NOTHING SOUNDS LIKE a bowling alley: the mounting centrifugal force as bowling balls approach the pins, the clap and clutter of the balls' initial impact, pins striking pins and pins falling. But far from being a cacophony, it's music to a bowler's ears.

And the smell. Not just one smell but a blend of smells—the smell of the oil on the lane, of the rosin used to dry hands, the disinfectant used on the house bowling shoes, grease from the food counter, cigarette smoke and beer. Each smell is pretty rotten on its own, but put them together and, ahhhhh, you're in a bowling alley. There's no other place like it in the world.

Trying to explain bowling only emphasizes how silly it is. But once you actually bowl you love it, and the silliness is transformed into an all-encompassing passion. I grew up near Rochester, New York, where everyone I know bowls. When I was a teenager, my favorite bowling alley was the Golden Greek's Tavern and Bowling Lanes. The dual-purpose facility was located in one building on Main Street in Scottsville, New York, a suburb of Rochester. It was a central location for the town, with both the tavern and the lanes doing great business. In the summer, the Greek, a guy named Mitch

Alapadikous, would cover the lanes with sheets of wood and have dances with live bands. The acoustics were never the greatest for the band—usually Muletrain, a group of local countrified hippies—because of the low ceiling. But the fun that was had was the finest kind.

Now I live in Brooklyn, the place the whole left side of the bowling lane is named after—the "Brooklyn Side." For most of the twentieth century, the bowling alley was as central to American communities as the ballpark, the malt shop, and the bandshell in the town square. It was a place where people met, dated, drank, exercised . . . you name it. For millions of bowlers, such as myself, there were huge chunks of life that seemed to revolve around the bowling alley.

HOW TO PLAY

So how do you bowl? Nothing could be easier. Using a heavy ball with holes drilled into it (for the thumb and the middle and ring fingers), you must knock down as many wooden pins as you can at the end of a sixty-foot lane.

To make things interesting, there are gutters on either side of the lane, so if the ball slips off the lane it goes into the gutter and stays there, guaranteeing that you'll knock down no pins with that ball. The lane is also heavily oiled, so that the slightest off-center rotation of the ball will cause it to change direction.

After your first ball, the mechanical pinsetter lifts the pins that are still standing, sweeps away any fallen pins that are in the way, and sets the upright pins back down where they were.

There are ten pins, each fifteen inches high, arranged in an equilateral triangle. A full set of ten pins is called a *rack*.

The area behind the pins, where fallen pins are swept, and where the ball ends up after each roll, is called the *pit*.

Beside the rack are walls called *sidewalls*, and pins are allowed to bounce off these walls and knock down other pins.

If you knock down all of the pins with your first ball, you've scored a *strike*. To have any chance of getting a strike, your ball must strike the front pin in the rack, the No. 1 pin, commonly referred to as the *headpin*.

If it takes both of your balls to knock down all the pins, you get a *spare*.

If there are still pins standing after both of your balls, you've scored a *miss*. A strike is better than a spare, which is better than a miss. How much better, you'll learn when you get to the chapter on keeping score.

GETTING TO THE LANES

The beautiful part about bowling is that you can do it during any season. And, no matter where you're located, there's a bowling alley nearby—almost always less than an hour away.

Finding the bowling center nearest you is as easy as picking up the Yellow Pages and making a few calls. You should always call an alley before you go. A lot of people bowl in leagues. They are members of teams with cheesy names like the Pinheads and Alleycats. Teams usually bowl three games apiece at the same time on the same night of the week. So if every Wednesday night is league night at your alley, that would be a lousy time to go and try to bowl for the first time.

GETTING SHOES

Okay, you get to the alley and there are plenty of lanes available. Don't worry if you don't have your own bowling ball. There are balls there for you to borrow—free of charge. But before you start searching for a ball, you have to rent shoes.

You cannot use your regular shoes. To bowl you must wear bowling shoes, which have special soles that do not harm the wood of the *approach area*, soles that are slick enough to allow you to slide into the release of your ball but have enough friction to keep you from sliding onto your derriere at the same time.

You'll have to give the person behind the shoe-rental counter your shoe size, along with one of your street shoes. He'll reach down into one of the many pigeonholes below desk level and pluck out a pair. These will be your shoes while you bowl.

Renting shoes is cheap, usually only a buck or two. If the thought of wearing a pair of shoes that have previously been worn by hundreds of sweaty strangers makes you queasy, don't worry. Bowling centers are very conscientious about the cleanliness of their shoes, which are disinfected and deodorized following every use. If that makes no difference to you and the thought still gives you the willies, perhaps your best bet is to buy your own pair. (They are sold at most sporting-goods stores.)

Once you've rented your shoes, try them on and make sure they fit before going to your lane. If they're uncomfortable, you can exchange them for another pair. You should have the same amount of room at the toe of your bowling shoes as you would in a normal pair of shoes.

FINDING A HOUSE BALL

Now it's time to find your ball. The "house balls," or the bowling balls that are there for bowlers who don't have their own, are kept on racks, usually at the back of the bowling center.

You'll need to determine how heavy a ball you want to use. This has been called being Goldilocks—that is, you need to find a ball that isn't not too heavy or too light but is *juuuuuuust* right. The idea is to use the heaviest possible ball that you can control. The heavier the ball, the easier it knocks down the pins. However, if the ball is too heavy, you'll miss your target. Beginners may have to take a few practice rolls before determining what is the best weight for them.

No matter how big or small you are, there is a perfect bowling ball for you. All bowling balls are the same size, however. Each is exactly 8.59 inches in diameter. However, the balls vary in weight from six to sixteen pounds. A small child can handle the six-pounder, and big, burly men are content with sixteen-pounders. Most balls are an even number of pounds—six, eight, ten, twelve, fourteen, and sixteen pounds being the most common weights, but 'tween weights are available as well.

Once you've determined the proper weight of your ball, you'll find that most house balls are color coded by weight, so almost all eight-pounders, for example, are dark red. If there are some peculiarly colored bowling balls on the rack, look at their surface. Usually, along with the manufacturer's logo and the initials of the poor fellow who originally bought the ball, is the weight of the ball.

Now that you know what weight you're looking for, you need to find a ball with the proper *span* for your hand. (The span is the distance between the thumbhole and the finger holes.) To do this, insert your thumb all the way into the thumbhole and then insert your middle two fingers as deeply as you can; the edge of the finger holes should be about a quarter-inch past the second knuckles.

Of course, the span of the ball is only one consideration. If the holes themselves are too large or too small for your fingers, it doesn't make any difference how far apart they are. The most important hole, sizewise, is the thumbhole. It is essential that the thumbhole not be too tight. If you have to work and work to get your thumb all the way into the hole, don't use that ball. You don't want to roll the ball down the lane with your thumb still attached. This disturbs the natural gyration of the ball, and makes a difficult-to-clean mess on the lane.

The thumb should fit into the hole with a "loose but not sloppy" fit. That means the thumb should slip in and out of the hole without any stress, rubbing gently along most of the inside of the hole. Too tight and you could hurt the thumb. Too loose and the thumb loses its ability to control the ball, adversely affecting your aim.

Your middle and ring fingers should also fit into their respective holes in a comfortable manner. A perfect fit here is not as important as the thumb fit, though. No house ball is going to give you a perfect fit. The rule with the fingers is: If it feels good, use it.

ANATOMY OF A LANE

Most bowlers like to get a walking start before they roll the ball down the lane. In order for them to do this, there is an *approach area*

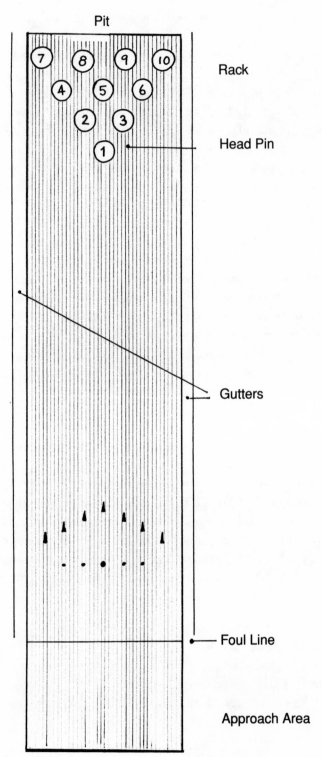

Pit

Rack

Head Pin

Gutters

Foul Line

Approach Area

Anatomy of a Lane

How To Build Your Own Bowling Lane

In case you want to build a bowling lane in your basement or backyard, here are the measurements you will need to know:

The overall length of your lane must be 62 feet, $10\frac{3}{16}$ inches from the foul line to the pit behind the pins. It must be within $\frac{1}{2}$ inch of 60 feet from the foul line to the center of the headpin, and 2 feet 10 $\frac{6}{16}$ ths inches from the center of the headpin to the pit. The lane must be between 41 and 42 inches wide. The lane will be made up of 39 boards across, of pine and maple wood. The lane (with gutters) has to be between 60 and 60 $\frac{1}{4}$ inches wide. The surface must be free of all continuous grooves. No more than $\frac{1}{25}$ th of an inch of groove depression is allowed. The approach area must be at least 15 feet long, made of maple, with grooves between the boards no deeper than $\frac{1}{4}$ inch. Obviously, the trick to building a lane is to get boards that will not warp. At all. Ever. The grooves between the boards are regulated to $\frac{1}{25}$ th of an inch. The margin of error for warpage is zilch. So be sure to consult with a lumber expert before buying your raw materials.

that measures fifteen feet by forty-two inches—the latter number being the width of the lane. Pilots, models, and pro bowlers sometimes refer to the approach area as the *runway*.

The bowler must deliver the ball from behind the *foul line*. The foul line is the borderline between the approach area and the lane. Crossing that lane negates all toppled pins. On either side of the lane are nine-inch-wide channels, more commonly referred to as the *gutters*. As in life, staying out of the gutter is very important in bowling.

KNOWING THE PINS BY NUMBER

If you've spent more than five minutes at a bowling alley, you've probably noticed that bowlers refer to the pins by number. (For

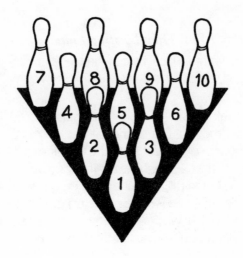

example, "That *blankety-blank* Ten Pin!") The pins are numbered from front to back and from left to right, so that when one bowler tells another that he has left a Seven-Ten split, his buddy knows exactly what he's talking about.

You don't have to memorize much in bowling, but memorizing these numbers is a good idea. It'll help you better understand every bowling story you hear or lesson you try to learn from now on. Above is a diagram of how the pins are numbered.

The One Pin is more commonly referred to as the headpin. Got 'em memorized? Good. Read on!

(Special note on style: When I refer to a pin by its number, it will be capitalized. So it will read, "After one ball there were five pins standing; one of them was the Five Pin.")

CHAPTER 2
Getting The Ball To The Pins

IN BOWLING, THE players take turns. You can use any method you like to determine who bowls first. Flip a coin, rock, paper, or scissors. Reverse order by bowling average, bowlers' weights. Whatever.

The first bowler rolls his first ball, then waits for the automatic pinsetter to reset the pins that are still standing. As the pinsetter is doing its job, an automatic ball returner has grabbed the ball, put it on a conveyor belt, and returned it to the approach area.

The first bowler rolls his second ball. This time the automatic pinsetter knocks down any pins that are still standing and sets down a fresh rack of ten pins for the second bowler.

You can have as many people bowling on one lane as you like, but it is recommended that no more than four use one lane at a time. If you are a party of eight, ask for two lanes. Otherwise, there will be long waits between each bowler's turns.

As I said, bowling is easy. You just roll the ball down the lane and knock down the pins. Couldn't be easier. Bowling *well* is a different story. To become a high-scoring bowler takes practice and concentration. So let's start from the beginning.

GETTING TO YOUR STANCE (SETTING UP)

The first thing you'll need to do before you actually bowl is assume your stance. Here are a few pointers and rules of etiquette to get you there.

1. Be ready to bowl when the person before you is finished. As he returns from bowling, you should greet him with at least one foot on the approach area. It's nice to give him a high five—or a low five, or touch knuckles, or whatever it is you do in your 'hood—if he made a strike or a spare.

2. Go to the ball rack and pick up your ball. If the ball rack has a built-in hot-air blower, you may want to briefly dry your hands before picking up the ball. Use two hands to lift the ball. Be careful that new balls rolling onto the ball rack do not hit your fingers. Do not stick your fingers into the ball's holes and pick up the ball with your fingers. Put your fingers into the holes after you have the ball cradled against your midsection with your non-bowling, or *balance*, hand.

3. Glance to either side of you to make sure that there is no one ready to bowl on your immediate right or left, then shift the ball so that it's resting in your palm and on the inside of your bowling wrist. The balance hand should remain on the ball, with your fingers extended to provide support.

4. Keep your eyes on the dots (or *range finders*) on the approach area; this will help you to align your shot. (We'll discuss the meaning of these dots in the next chapter.)

5. Square yourself to the lane. Face the pins directly. Stand with your knees ever so slightly bent. Your back should be straight, your shoulders and hips perpendicular to the lane. Position your feet close together—two or three inches apart—and so that your heels and toes form a square. It's easy to keep your feet square using the boards on the approach area. Now you're ready to go.

Here's what a proper stance should look like.

THE APPROACH

Most people address the lane with their feet a few inches apart, eyes on the target, and the ball held in both hands at mid-chest level. Others prefer to start the ball in both hands down at their hip. The latter stance is called the *midline ball setup*. It tends to keep the delivery more compact because the ball has less distance to travel to get to the start of the *backswing*. The midline stance will shorten the time it takes to get the ball to the release, and is often assumed by bowlers whose legs reach the *finish* before their arm does.

We will be discussing the *four-step approach* here, starting with the ball at mid-chest. Starting the ball higher allows gravity to do just a little bit more of the work for you, building up some energy even before the difficult part of your backswing begins. (Those who have very long arms sometimes add a fifth step because it makes it easier for them to finish with their arm and their legs at the same time. People with shorter arms or shorter backswings will sometimes use only three steps, but four is the norm.) You should not think about your steps being of any particular length. Your stride should be the same as it would be if you were walking down the street at a relaxed pace.

To begin the *approach*, your eyes should be on the target, whether it be the pins or the range finders. Keep your eyes on the target at all times during the approach and *delivery*. After you've made sure that the lanes are clear on either side, there's no reason to look away from the target. Focus and lock in.

Your first movement is to push the ball out, straight forward and slightly down.

The right foot then follows with your first step.

As you begin your second step, bend forward slightly at the waist. Let the ball swing freely from the shoulder past your hip, back behind you. Keep a relaxed, loose grip on the ball and a straight, loose wrist. This will keep you free of muscle tension in your hand and arm as you swing the ball. You are beginning to build up momentum toward the pins and the foul line.

As you stride forward with your third step, your right foot is in front and your bowling arm is straight behind you. (Some bowlers find that they have trouble completing their backswing, probably because they're anxious to get the ball on its way, so that the ball gets to the floor before the legs are ready for it. A good way to assure that this doesn't happen is to pause for a nanosecond at the top of the backswing, a deliberate hitch, then move into your downswing.)

As you start forward with the ball, you also begin your fourth and final step.

Remember, your arm should swing down in a straight arc, no matter how much curve you want to put on the ball. Do not swing the bowling arm across your body. This will cause the ball to miss to the left and can result in injuries to the shoulder and elbow.

LOW AND SLOW

The ball passes your right leg as your fourth step finishes. You are bent forward at the waist no more than twenty degrees. Your center of gravity is low. That is, your hips are down. Your eyes remain on the target. (Do not let your arm swing wildly. Your mantra should be: Low and slow . . . low and slow . . . low and . . .)

1.

2.

3.

The approach, broken down step by step. **(continued)**

Your left toe should slide right up to but *never, ever go over* the foul line. You will swing the ball out over the foul line slightly and release it just before it touches the lane. As you release, your right foot comes up and wraps around behind you slightly.

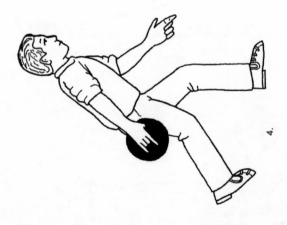

4.

(continued) The approach, broken down step by step.

6.

5.

(continued) *The approach, broken down step by step.*

Getting the Ball To the Pins

15

A PLETHORA OF REASONS NOT TO FOUL

A legal delivery means rolling the ball toward the pins without any part of your body, *especially your toe*, going over the foul line. This does not mean that your whole body has to be behind the foul line when you release the ball; you just can't *touch* the lane beyond that line. Your lead toe should slide up to within about an inch of the line while your bowling hand releases the ball out over the lane, well beyond the line.

Delivering the ball in this manner takes some practice. If you lose your balance, lean forward and touch down on the lane after releasing the ball, you've sacrificed your entire frame—even if you foul on the first ball.

Besides, touching the lane beyond the foul line is apt to make you an oily mess. If you're wearing house shoes, many bowling centers will demand that you change into new ones if you step over the foul line. If you're wearing your own shoes, you'll be advised to clean them off thoroughly before continuing.

Having oil on the bottoms of your bowling shoes is dangerous. The shoes are designed to be low-friction with the lane wood as it is, because you're supposed to slide up to the foul line with your lead toe. Any other substance can turn you into Jackie Gleason on roller skates—only *you'll* end up hurting yourself.

There are people who've been stupid enough to bring talcum powder or ashes with them to the bowling center, thinking that applying these to the soles of their shoes will help give them a nice slide. The results are disastrous—a nice concussion in one case.

FOLLOW THROUGH, BUT DON'T "MUSCLE" THE BALL

To add power to your release, accelerate your arm during your downswing, then decelerate during your follow-through. In other words, do not jerk your arm to a stop once you've released the ball. And don't continue to push with your arm after the ball is gone. Slowly bring your arm to a stop, as if you were softly pressing on the brake pedal to stop a car. At the same time, keep the arm moving in exactly the same arc that it was in before the release.

If you continue to accelerate your arm past the release point, you'll end up doing what's called *muscling* the ball—a mistake that's frequently accompanied by a grunt of exertion. Your ball will skid down the lane a ways before it starts rolling, thus decreasing its effectiveness as a pin-buster.

POSING

Here's a good way to make sure that you're following through in a straight arc, thus assuring that the ball travels along the intended path. Continue your follow-through until you can put your bowling thumb on your nose. Touch the tip of your thumb to the tip of your nose, extend the fingers, and wiggle them.

Seriously, though, you may have noticed that a lot of good bowlers appear to be posing—holding still like a statue—after they complete their delivery. This isn't vanity but an important part of the rhythm and cadence of their delivery. It also assures the bowler that she has completed her follow-through.

Balance

No matter how many steps you use during your approach to the foul line, it's important to maintain your balance throughout the process. Some bowlers have difficulty with this, and the reason is obvious: The bowler is carrying a twelve- to sixteen-pound ball on one side of her body and nothing on the other.

In order to counteract the weight on your bowling side, stick your non-bowling arm straight out to your side during your approach. That arm will tend to come up naturally as you bowl, but try to get it up so that it's parallel with your shoulders. That will help keep the ball from pulling your upper body out of alignment and keep your shoulders square.

Another thing to watch, if balance is a problem, is the position of your lead toe at the point of release. Your lead foot should be perpendicular to the foul line. If that foot is at an angle, your balance

Rudy "Revs" Kasimakis poses at the end of his delivery—and the crowd goes, "Oooooooh."

will be adversely affected and the accuracy of your shot will be diminished.

If you finish properly, you'll be in a position known as *sitting tall*, with your back straight and tilted forward only slightly, your center of gravity kept low because of the bend in your knees. The idea is to "project" the ball out over the lane, lifting with your fingertips at the last possible instant, so that you achieve a perfect roll. A perfectly rolled bowling ball will fully rotate every twenty-seven inches on its way down the lane. Mere mortals can only hope for that kind of a roll. The rest of us have some degree of *skid*.

The idea is to *not* drop the ball and to make sure that your fingertips—and not your thumb—are the last thing to touch the ball. If you can accomplish this, chances are you're getting a pretty good roll. A well-rolled ball sounds great on the lane and has a more dynamic impact.

(A note to all the lefties out there: We've been discussing the delivery of a right-handed bowler. If you want the lesson to apply to you, simply read this section in the mirror. No, seriously, the principles described in this chapter work exactly the same way for lefties. Simply substitute rights for lefts and vice versa.)

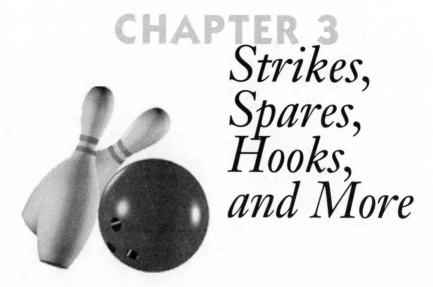

CHAPTER 3

Strikes, Spares, Hooks, and More

OKAY, WE'VE LEARNED how to pick out equipment, and the proper way to approach and deliver the bowling ball to the pins. Now the question is, Where do I aim—and how?

On the first ball, you have only one goal: Get a strike! To do that, you have to aim between the One and the Three Pin. Remember, in order to get a strike, you *must* hit the headpin. (Lefties, aim for the gap between the One and the Two Pin.) If you hit only the headpin, however, you will usually get a *split*, a nasty result that we'll be discussing later. Getting a strike is, for most people, the most exciting thing you can do when bowling.

STRIKES

Why do people bowl with a curved ball, or a *hook*? The reason is: strikes. To get strikes with any kind of regularity, it's preferable to hit the *pocket*—again, the area between the One and Three Pins for a righty and between the One and Two Pins for a lefty—at an angle rather than straight on (see illustration on following page).

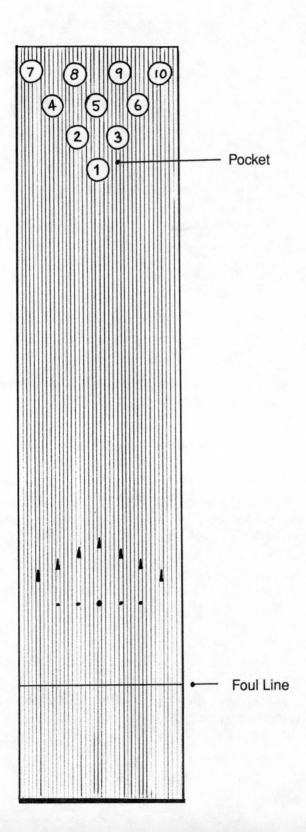

Pocket

Foul Line

Since it's illegal to bank the ball off another object, the only way to get the ball to hit the pins from the appropriate angle of attack is to hook it in there. It is tons more difficult to throw strikes with a straight ball, although it is possible—especially if you make strong pocket hits and start the ball from the edge rather than from the center of the lane.

Although it may not look that way to the naked eye, every bowling ball changes direction when it first impacts the pins. When a right-handed bowler hits the right pocket, the ball always hits the headpin first, because it is so far in front. This contact deflects the ball to the right. In order for a strike to occur, the ball must hit the Five Pin, the pin in the center of the pack. If that original deflection causes the ball to miss the Five, chances are there will be pins still standing when the dust clears.

HOW TO THROW A HOOK

Assuming you want to throw a hook, you will rotate your hand and wrist so that your hand moves from the bottom to the right side, or outside of the ball. The farther your hand is toward the right-hand side of the ball at the point of release, the more that imbalance will affect the rotation of the ball, and the more the ball will hook. Big hookers release the ball with their hand on the extreme right of the ball so that they finish up their delivery looking as if they were about to shake hands.

To put it another way, throwing a hook involves rotating your thumb counterclockwise during your downswing. You do this by turning your hand, wrist, and forearm inward, also rotating counterclockwise. The farther your thumb moves to the left, the shorter the axis of rotation on the ball will be once it starts rolling, and the farther left the ball will hook on its way down the lane.

When you throw a straight ball, the ball will roll off the ring and middle fingers almost simultaneously. When you throw a hook, the middle finger does most of the work, since—with the counterclockwise rotation of your wrist—the middle finger has become the top finger.

Bowlers who throw a hook go about it in a couple of different ways. One is the *outside line shot*, in which you start the ball straight down the lane, but on the right side, allowing the ball to hook into the pocket (see illustration below). The other is the *inside line shot*, in which you start the ball on the left side of the lane and roll it across the lane on a diagonal to the right side, so that it can then hook into the pocket for a devastating strike (see illustration on page 25).

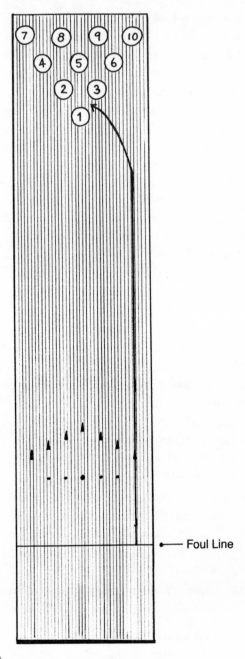

Foul Line

Outside line shot

You don't necessarily need to get married to either technique, since the one you use may be determined by the condition of the lanes. The important thing is consistency. If you can throw the same hook every time, then you know where you have to start it out in order to get it to finish where it belongs.

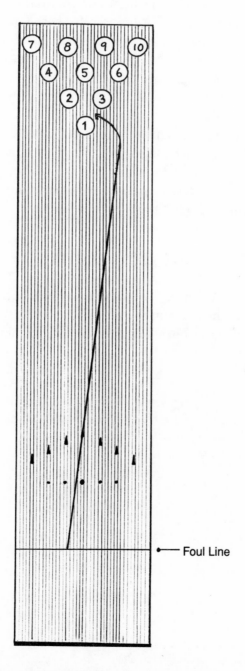

Foul Line

Inside line shot

And the way to get a consistent hook is to have a consistent delivery. If your natural hook isn't getting along with the lane, how do you compensate? Adjust with the angle of release? Not necessarily. Sometimes it's better to adjust to the lane by altering the speed of your ball, while keeping the gyro effect on the ball the same.

The speed of your ball determines where on the lane your ball will hook the sharpest. The harder you throw the ball, the farther down the track its *break point* will be. The ideal location for a strike ball's break point is about six feet from the headpin, so if your hook is consistently crossing over, more speed might be the answer. If your hits are consistently to the right of the target, take a little of the mustard off and that might work.

(Special note regarding illustrations on pages 24 and 25: An actual bowling lane is much longer and narrow than shown here. We have shortened and widened the lane to make illustrations easier to see. Use these illustrations as general demonstrations of an inside- and outside-line shot. Do not use them as templates for precision.)

HOW TO USE THE DOTS AND ARROWS

On the approach area there are five dots, a large dot in alignment with the center of the lane (on the twentieth board), with two small spots on either side five boards apart—just like the pins. They look like this:

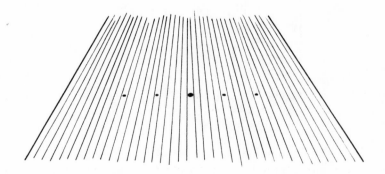

There are lanes that have one more spot on either end, five boards beyond these, so that there are seven spots—one representing each of the visible, pins when each frame starts: the Seven-Four-Two-One-Three-Six-and-Ten pins. Once you've figured out where you need to start your feet for you and the ball to finish in the right place, the dots will help you start with your toes on precisely the correct boards during your stance. If your first balls are hitting the headpin too *high*—in other words, too far to the left for a right-handed bowler (getting "too much headpin," it's called)—simply start one or two boards farther right, use the same delivery, and the ball should hit the strike pocket perfectly the next time. If your hits are too *light*, too far to the right, move your feet to the left when you start and keep everything else the same.

The arrows are painted on the lane itself and look like this:

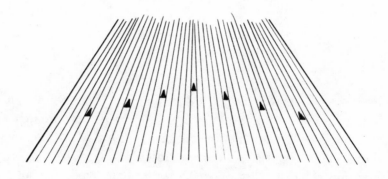

Although the arrows help all bowlers aim at the pins better—since they align with the front pins, the Four-Two-One-Three-Six pins—they are particularly valuable to bowlers with a hook, as these bowlers need a reference point in order to know where the ball is at a particular point down the lane. Most right-handed hookers (pardon the expression) find that the second arrow on the right is the one to go for.

A WORD OF ENCOURAGEMENT

Most people think that you have to be a pro bowler, or at least a fanatic bowler, to string a bunch of strikes together. But this isn't true. All you need to do is get in a groove.

Just a few years ago, I was bowling on Long Island with friends when a college buddy of mine named Scott Frommer got hot. Scott is a 140–150 bowler (i.e., extremely mediocre), and he doesn't even really have a formal average because he bowls so infrequently. On this occasion, though, Scott could do no wrong, and he started one game out with nine consecutive strikes. By the time his tenth frame began, everyone in the bowling alley knew what was going on and was watching. At that point, the magic wore off and he returned to being a mere mortal.

But keep Scott's story in mind the next time you start out with two in a row or three in a row. Just do the same thing every time and you, too, could join the ranks of the immortals who have bowled a *perfect game*.

SPARES

Some bowlers feel that picking a difficult spare is more fun than getting a strike. There are several reasons for this. There are many different spare balls, but only one strike ball. Plus, with so many pins flying on your first ball, it can be difficult to see what's going on. When you're picking a spare, on the other hand, you can usually see exactly which pins get knocked down by the ball and which get knocked down by other pins.

Unfortunately, picking easy spares can offer some of the sport's most nerve-racking moments. Say you're picking a single Seven or Ten Pin. It looks so simple, but two psychological factors threaten to take over if you let them:

1. The second shot is very, very different from the first.

2. Gee, that pin sure is close to the channel.

The difference between coming up with a strike and coming up with a lone Seven or Ten Pin is this: With the strike, the pins fly to the back of the pit sideways—or spinning like a propeller on the loose. With the standing Ten Pin, the pins flew through head- or tailfirst. Can you alter your game so that all of the pins you knock down go sideways?

No.

It's a matter of luck.

DON'T CRY. PICK IT.

The key is not to let the *leave* (that is, the pins left standing) bother you. It's all part of the game. In a perfect world, all leaves would be strikes. But the world ain't perfect. Okay, you didn't get a strike. Don't let your emotions affect your game. You've still got work to do. Even if your first ball was perfect and you deserved a strike in every way, keep your cool. Don't cry. Pick it. Missing that leave turns bad luck into disaster.

TWO DIFFERENT DELIVERIES?

There are two schools of thought regarding whether you should use two different deliveries when bowling—one for strikes and one for spares.

If you're a bowler who is excellent at getting strikes and excellent at picking spares, then ignore all of this. If you only feel comfortable rolling the ball one way, or if you're afraid that two swings will lead to body-memory indecision at some key moment in a match, then see a muscle shrink and call me in the morning. Everybody else, consider trying two different deliveries—one for the first ball and one for the second. Concentrate more on leverage and power when you bowl for a strike. To achieve this, take a long backswing. Also, put as much hook on the ball as you can control.

However, when you go for a spare you don't need power, just accuracy. Shorten your backswing and keep your hand at the bottom of the ball at the point of release. In other words, do not rotate your hand counterclockwise. The axis of rotation should be very close to the "equator," or largest circumference, of the ball. The ball should roll straight as an arrow all the way to the pins. This should serve to increase your accuracy, which is important because, with some difficult spares, a quarter of an inch can make all the difference.

Some rules regarding spares are easy to remember:

1. If the headpin is still standing, another strike ball usually does the trick. However, there are exceptions: A One-Ten leave will necessitate that the ball strike the left side of the headpin, causing the pin to kick back and to the right so that it takes out the Ten. In order to do that, a bowler's ball must cross over onto the left-hand side, or the "Brooklyn side" of the lane.

2. Always aim at the pin closest to you—that is, the front-most pin.

3. Always aim so that your *ball* will knock down the most pins possible.

Other rules are more difficult to execute. For example:

4. If there is are *soldiers* standing (one pin directly behind the other so that only the front pin is visible from the approach area), yet there is a pin to the left that needs to be picked up as well—the One-Two-Five leave is the most common example—remember to hit the ball high on the headpin, so that the One takes out the Five. A *crossover* hit, or a hit that is too light, will almost always knock down the One and Two, but the soldier, the Five Pin, will usually continue to stand at attention.

PICKING THE TEN PIN

A bowler throwing a straight ball can pick the Ten Pin in any way he chooses. He could roll the ball directly up the far-right edge of the lane. He could start at the far left of the approach area and roll the ball diagonally at the pin. As long as his aim is true, the ball will hit the pin and knock it down.

For righties with a hook, the options are more limited. You must start at the far left of the lane and roll the ball into a direction that, if the ball were to go straight, would send it in the gutter. That takes some guts, and you have to trust your hook. Obviously, it will take some practice before you figure out where on the approach area you must start and which arrow you must aim for, but once you get it, you'll have it. It's like riding a bicycle.

The Ten Pin is such a common leave that alleys often have a groove to them. But, be aware, if you try to pick a Ten Pin with a hook on a freshly oiled lane your ball may not hook as much as you expect. Chances are it will slide off the dance floor completely and go splashing into the sewer. Adjust!

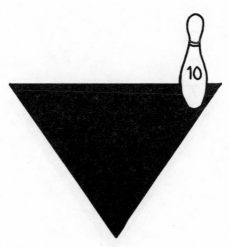

The Ten-Pin leave

Lefties who want to learn how to pick a Ten Pin should read the section below for righties on how to pick the Seven Pin. Lefties learning to pick the Seven Pin should read the above tips for righties picking the Ten Pin. Left-handers will have slightly more difficulty picking a Seven Pin than righties do picking a Ten Pin because there is usually no groove to the pin.

PICKING THE SEVEN PIN

Although, technically, you could pick a Seven Pin by rolling a straight ball up the left-most edge of the lane, I wouldn't recommend this technique. It necessitates an approach that is actually between alleys. The ball rack could get in the way, and you could get in the way of someone bowling on the next lane. (Lefties are welcome to do it this way.)

No, the best way to knock down a lone Seven Pin is to bowl diagonally across the alley. A simple rule of thumb is: Release your ball at the exact center of the lane, and aim for the third arrow from the left—one arrow over from the center. Those two points determine a straight line that takes the ball through the Seven Pin.

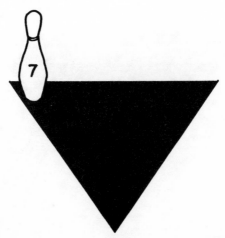

The Seven-Pin leave

SEVEN-TEN BLUES AND OTHER SPLIT DECISIONS

A *split* is any leave in which the remaining pins are not conveniently clustered in one place but instead split up into two areas of the rack. The most notorious and difficult split to pick is the *Seven-Ten split*.

The other split that makes the top of every bowler's least-wanted list is the *Double Pinochle*, or the *Four-Seven/Six-Ten split*.

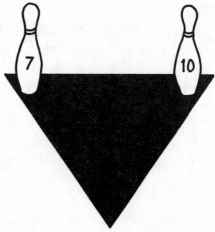

The Seven-Ten split

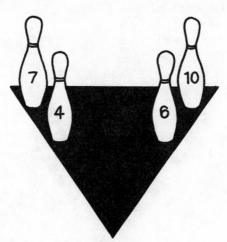

The Double Pinochle

Splits like these are generally caused when a bowler's first ball strays away from the strike pocket and hits the headpin alone. This is called a *high hit*.

Picking splits is the most difficult task a bowler must face. It is so difficult, in fact, that there are many very good bowler's who are lousy when it comes to picking splits.

There are two reasons for this:

1. It's very difficult.
2. The bowler is so mad that he got a split in the first place that he isn't concentrating properly on his second shot.

As for the first reason, the very fact that picking splits is hard is what makes doing it correctly one of the game's biggest thrills. There is no excuse for the second reason. Bowlers must learn to control their emotions. Just as a bowler who has rolled eleven straight strikes must take a deep breath and remain calm for his last ball of the game, so a bowler who has suffered a split must remain calm and make the best of a bad situation.

In order to pick a split, you must not only hit the target pin but hit it in such a fashion that it kicks in the proper direction and knocks down the pin or pins on the other side of the split. A bowler picking a *Five-Ten split*, for example, must hit the Five Pin on the

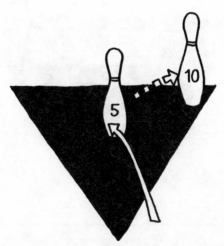

Picking the Five-Ten split

left-hand side, so that the pin kicks right and takes out the Ten. A bowler going after a Five-Seven split must hit the Five on the right-hand side so that the pin flies left and knocks over the Seven.

To pick the Seven-Ten split, a right-handed bowler will probably roll his second ball toward the Seven Pin, attempting to hit as little of that pin as possible on the left side—that is, a "thin" hit— so that the target pin will slide directly across the pit and knock down the Ten. Since this attempt often results in missing the Ten Pin altogether, some bowlers may opt not to pick the split at all but, rather, to "play it safe," cut their losses, and knock down one of the two pins.

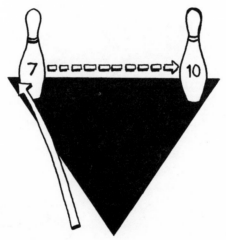

Picking the Seven-Ten split

The Double Pinochle is even more difficult to pick, as the Six Pin must be hit in such a fashion that it not only hits the Four Pin but knocks the Four into the Seven. The ball will take out the Ten Pin.

Most bowlers will settle for taking out one-half of the Double Pinochle rather than trying to pick it. As in the case of the Seven-Ten split, aiming to hit the Six Pin so thinly often results in missing it altogether.

A SECOND, MORE DETAILED APOLOGY TO LEFTIES

Lefties must take all the above advice and reverse it, sort of. There are differences in the game for lefties that must be addressed. Right-handed bowlers have the benefit of a groove caused by bowler after bowler's throwing a strike ball with a similar line. Southpaws do not have that benefit. Fewer than one out of every ten bowlers rolls the ball from the portside, so they are always bowling on a side of the lane that is seldom used. As a result, they rarely get to bowl on a "dry" lane, or a lane that encourages a good hook.

There are people who believe that left-handed bowlers "throw a natural hook." Bowling is not the only sport in which southpaws have mythologically been granted mystical powers to bend the path of a moving sphere. The myth, it should be noted, has no basis in science. Many left-handers, however, do choose to throw a big hook, starting the ball at the far-left edge of the lane. Perhaps this is because, unlike righties, they do not have to worry about bowling under different conditions each time out: Things tend to stay the same over there on the left.

CHAPTER 4

How To Keep Score: A Dying Art

I FEAR THAT scorekeeping in bowling is going to become a lost skill. I fear for a generation of bowlers who, nineteen points behind with three frames left to go, don't have a clue what they need to do to win.

On the other side of the coin, it's important to know just how badly one's opponent needs to do in order to lose. All that suspense gone! Still, to get maximum enjoyment out of bowling, you need to know how to keep score.

And why is scorekeeping turning into a dinosaur? Because today, when you go to the lanes, you don't have to keep score. A computer does it for you. (The computerized scoring system for bowling centers was patented by James P. Cullen in 1990.)

For those of you who are too young to recall, this is what it was like before the computers and the bells and whistles were installed:

When you got your lane and your shoes, the guy or gal behind the counter wrote your lane number at the top of your score sheet, circled it, and handed the sheet back to you. Back at your alley, you clipped your score sheet to the table—which was very similar to the ones they have today except there was a slanted desk, and a couple of circular holes for drinks and maybe an ashtray. You clipped your score sheet to the top of the desk under a clip like the kind you might find on a clipboard. There were pencils there for you, and they weren't the cheap little stubby pencils you might get at a miniature golf course. These were full-length No. 2 pencils with erasers! Nine times out of ten they were sharp, too. Your score sheet looked like this:

NAME	1	2	3	4	5	6	7	8	9	10
1										
2										
3										
4										
5										
6										
7										
8										
9										
10										

SCORING A GAME

And this was how you kept score:

Scorekeeping consists of counting the pins that were knocked down and adding bonuses when all ten pins have been knocked down. If you get a spare, knocking down all the pins with both rolls, you get those ten, plus the number of pins that were knocked down with your first ball in the next frame.

Say I start in the first frame and *break for nine*—that is, knock down nine pins with my first ball—then make my spare. In the upper portion of the first big box, next to my name, I write a nine. I put a diagonal slash through the little box to show that I had a spare. I don't put any number at all in the lower portion of the big box. Because I got a spare, I won't know my score for the first frame until after my first ball in the second frame.

In the second frame, I break for nine again. Now I know my first-frame score. I get ten for the ten pins I knocked down, plus nine for the first ball in the second frame: nineteen.

My first frame score would look like this:

NAME	1	2	3	4	5	6	7	8	9	10
1 Michael	9⧄ / 19	9								
2										
3										
4										
5										
6										
7										
8										
9										
10										

On my second ball in the second frame, I miss the pin and have an "open frame." No bonus. The number of pins I got on the first ball goes in front of the little box in the second frame and I put a dash in the little box to show I had an open frame, or failed to knock down all the pins.

Scorekeepers generally don't use a zero, as it is too easily confused with a circle, which is the symbol for a split. My score for the first two frames is twenty-eight, since nineteen plus nine equals twenty-eight. The score sheet would look like this:

NAME	1	2	3	4	5	6	7	8	9	10
1 Michael	9 ⟋ 19	9 — 28								
2										
3										
4										
5										
6										
7										
8										
9										
10										

If I had knocked down eight pins with my first ball and one with my second, my score would be the same but my score sheet would have an eight in front of the little box and a one inside it.

Now, in the third, fourth, and fifth frames I get strikes. Strikes are scored by placing an *X* in the little box. (Some fancy scorekeepers color in sections of the little box, two sides of the *X* for a strike and one-half of the slashed box for a spare because it makes it easier to count "marks"—which is what strikes and spares are called, precisely for that reason.)

Strikes, as they should, earn the best bonus of all. I get the ten points for the pins I knocked down, plus—as a bonus—the number of pins I get on my next two balls, regardless of whether they take place in the same frame. Therefore in the third frame I get ten pins for those that I knocked down, plus ten for the pins I knocked down with my first ball in the fourth frame, and ten for those I felled in the fifth.

So I scored thirty points in the third frame, bringing my total to fifty-eight. I cannot yet score my fourth frame, because I have yet to roll two balls since my fourth-frame strike, so I don't know what my bonus will be. Since a strike earns me ten points plus what I get on my next two rolls, my score in the fourth frame is ten points for my strike, plus the total number of pins I knock down on my next two balls. Here's how my score sheet looks now:

NAME	1	2	3	4	5	6	7	8	9	10
1 *Michael*	9 ◿ 19	9 ⊢ 28	☒ 58	☒	☒					
2										
3										
4										
5										
6										
7										
8										
9										
10										

SCORING THE LAST FRAME

Let's move briefly away from our hypothetical game—to one of my favorite subjects: perfection. I choose this not because it's every bowler's goal but because it helps us to understand the trickiest part of scoring a game, the tenth and final frame.

As we've learned, the maximum number of points you can score in one frame is thirty, and you do it by stringing together strikes. Thus a perfect ten-frame, twelve-strike game gives you 300 points. Wait a second, you say. Why isn't it 280? That would be thirty points apiece for the first nine frames, and then ten for knocking down all the pins in the tenth, or 280. Well, the tenth frame is different.

You get your bonus for your spare and strike to open the tenth, even though it's the last frame. Therefore if you get a spare in the tenth, you get one more ball and you get credit for the number of pins you knock down with that ball, added to the ten you've already felled in the tenth. If you start the tenth with a strike, you get two bonus balls. So a maximum of thirty points can be scored in the final frame as well if one strike is followed by two bonus strikes.

If you fail to knock down all ten pins with your first two balls in the tenth, your game is over. To score twenty-seven points in the tenth frame, you would *have* to bowl two strikes and get seven pins with your final ball. To score nineteen, you would need a spare followed by a nine-pin break, or a strike followed by two balls in which a total of nine pins were knocked down.

If you start your frame with a spare and get a strike with your one bonus ball, you get twenty points in the final frame. An easy shortcut when scorekeeping is that, no matter what frame it is, a spare following a strike or a strike following a spare is always worth twenty points.

BACK TO OUR GAME

In my sixth frame, my first ball hit up too high on the headpin and the result was the Seven-Ten split. I put an eight with a circle around it to show that it's a split. I picked up the Ten Pin, so I put a one in the little box. I scored only nine points in the sixth frame.

My eight pins knocked down on the first ball of my sixth frame means I can now add up my total for the fourth frame. I get fifty-eight plus ten for the ten pins knocked down, plus nineteen pins for my bonus (the sum of my next two balls). That gives me eighty-six in the fourth.

In the fifth, I get ten for pins knocked down plus nine for my next two balls.

In the sixth, I get just the nine pins knocked down, which means that, after six frames bowled, I have 114 points.

My score sheet now looks like this:

NAME	1	2	3	4	5	6	7	8	9	10
1 Michael	7 ⟋ 19	9 - 28	✕ 58	✕ 86	✕ 105	⑧ 1 114				
2										
3										
4										
5										
6										
7										
8										
9										
10										

Bowling Etiquette

1. Be ready when it's your turn to bowl.

2. Always yield to the bowlers on your immediate left and right if they are ready to bowl.

3. Roll the ball, don't loft it. It's bad bowling, it hurts the lane—and it's rude.

4. Wait until the pinsetting equipment has come to a stop before you bowl. Folks who try to time their shot so that it hits the pins a nanosecond after the machine goes up are asking for a hefty damages suit.

5. If you accidentally step over the foul line and get "lane dressing" on your shoes, wipe them off immediately before bowling again.

6. Try to keep your post-strike celebrations physical rather than verbal. A little fist pumping and body English is expected, but loud exclamations may startle a nearby bowler.

7. For those who indulge, the fifth frame of each game is the "beer" frame. The bowler who knocks down the fewest pins on his or her first ball buys. (In some neighborhoods, any frame in which everyone gets a strike but you is the beer frame and you buy.)

8. Be a good loser.

9. Be a good winner.

To keep things simple, and to better reflect reality, I got nothing but strikes the rest of the way, so my final score was . . . think . . . right! 234! Not bad. We've now covered all of the rules of score-keeping. Learn them and you'll never have to rely on a computer to keep score for you again. (You'll also know when the computer makes a mistake, but don't get me started.)

My complete game score looks like this:

NAME	1	2	3	4	5	6	7	8	9	10
1 Michael	9 ⟋ 19	9 ⎿⎻ 28	☒ 58	☒ 86	☒ 105	⑧ 1 114	☒ 144	☒ 174	☒ 204	☒ ☒ ☒ 234
2										
3										
4										
5										
6										
7										
8										
9										
10										

BOTTOM LINE

STRIKE: ten plus the next two balls;
SPARE: ten plus the next ball;
MISS: pins knocked down plus doodly-squat.

CHAPTER 5
Equipment and Accessories

BALLS

WHICH BOWLERS SHOULD own their own bowling ball? Well, technically, the answer is all of them. There isn't a bowler alive who wouldn't benefit from having his own personally designed ball.

Using a house ball, with its approximation of your fingers' girth and the span of your hand, causes you to compensate in one way or another with every roll. Over the long haul, this can lead to very sore hands and perhaps even injuries. The first time you use a customized ball that literally fits you like a glove, you can never go back to using a house ball.

Of course, that's the idealistic perspective—and there are many bowlers who simply don't go bowling often enough and who haven't the expendable income to justify purchasing their own bowling ball. We'll let them slide. The rest of you, pay attention.

THE PROPER WEIGHT

As I stated earlier, your bowling ball should be as heavy as you can control. The heavier the ball, the more momentum it builds on the lane and the greater the force with which it hits the pins. However, if a ball is too heavy for you, your ability to hit a target with it will decrease. One thing to consider: It has been shown that an average bowler can handle a customized bowling ball that is two to three pounds heavier than the heaviest house ball he or she can control. For example, a woman who uses a ten-pound house ball should be able to handle a twelve-pound ball drilled to fit her.

Recent studies have also shown that a fourteen-pound ball, if thrown correctly, has almost the same strike-producing capability as a sixteen-pound ball. So male bowlers shouldn't feel that they *have* to use the sixteen-pounder, because that's what manly men do and that's the only way to get maximum strike potential. It ain't necessarily so. Many men find the sixteen-pounder stressful on their joints. For them, a switch to a lighter ball would be recommended. If you're throwing a good bowling ball, one that hooks nicely and has good roll, fourteen pounds is all you need.

MATERIALS USED TO MAKE BOWLING BALLS

Since 1960, there have been four major changes in coverstock material for bowling balls. Up until the days of the Beatles and *Beach Party* movies, rubber balls were your only choice. (An interesting sidebar here is the fact that no bowling balls were manufactured during World War II because all rubber was needed for the war effort.)

During the 1970s, the *polyester* ball was introduced, perhaps so the balls matched the leisure suits the guys were wearing down the street at the dance hall. What sets the polyester or plastic ball apart is that its performance doesn't fluctuate with changing lane conditions as much as it would with balls made of other materials The polyester ball tends to roll straight with very little hook, no matter how much oil is on the lane.

The biggest factor in the variation of lane conditions that the bowler has to worry about is oil. If you bowl immediately after the lanes are oiled, you know that it can affect everything from your footing to your hook. The drier the lane is—that is, the less oil there is on it—the more a ball will hook. More oil tends to lessen the effect of the ball's rotation on its path. Therefore polyester balls may be good for you if you throw the sort of big hook that's difficult to control on a dry lane. Also, plastic balls tend to be cheaper than balls made of other materials.

In the 1980s, *urethanes* replaced polyester as the material of choice. The '90s brought further improvements in bowling-ball material with the development of *reactive urethane*. Urethane is also the material of choice for some bowlers when the lanes are dry. The urethane ball provides a more controlled, uniform hook, so that a big hooker is more apt to be able to keep his hook reined in under dry-lane conditions. As a result of this improved accuracy from the urethane ball, modern bowling scores have skyrocketed.

Both urethane balls and reactive urethane balls can be drilled to suit your needs, with adjustments made depending on how much hook and skid you get on your ball. Of course, many bowlers prefer urethane balls to reactive urethane balls because of the difference in cost. Urethane is much better suited to the family bowler, while reactive balls are still priced for bowlers who are looking for a return on their investment. In other words, pros and semipros. Urethane balls are also easier to maintain and last longer than their reactive counterparts. The reactives, while powerful, have not been known for their longevity. (We'll discuss how to lengthen the life of a reactive ball a little later.)

So what's the advantage of the reactive ball, which was first introduced to the bowling pro shop about six years ago? Plenty. The main characteristic of the reactive ball—or the reactive resin ball, as it is sometimes called—is its "tackiness." The tacky, or soft, surface actually grips the lane, giving the ball an increased hook potential. The gripping power maximizes the tightness of the ball's roll, and therefore its centrifugal force, which actually increases the ball's hitting power.

The reactive ball is so dynamic that it actually lessens the need for accuracy. This is especially true on a bowler's first ball. It's no longer necessary for most bowlers to hit a precise point to get a strike. Rather, there is a range that a bowler only needs to be within.

As with other balls, the amount of hook you get with your reactive ball can be adjusted by your pro-shop when it's drilled. A smart bowler will inform his pro-shop representative of his own bowling style as well as the typical conditions of the lanes where he bowls before he gets his ball drilled.

One frequently heard complaint regarding the reactive resin ball is that it is occasionally less than effective when it comes to making spares. Although it isn't possible for all bowlers to bring more than one ball with them to the lane, it has been recommended that bowlers use the reactive resin ball for their first ball, their strike ball, when the groove the ball must stay in is fairly predictable and a monster hook can be thrown without fear. Spares are peculiar animals, however, and involve rolling the ball on portions of the lane that are used less frequently and with lane conditions that are less predictable. For spares, therefore, some prefer a plastic ball for a straighter line and better accuracy regardless of lane conditions.

New products that raise eyebrows are hitting the market all the time. For example, when the Brunswick Pro Staffer ball won five of the first six PBA tournaments, folks started to take notice. The Pro Staffer is called a *proactive ball*. A new coverstock material developed by the Bayer Corporation, in conjunction with Brunswick, proactive features a microscopic texture in the surface of the bowling ball. It appears to be smooth, but that's an illusion.

You bowling-center operators can relax. The experts did tests and found that the textured surface of the proactive ball doesn't harm the lanes. But that texture does allow the ball to track evenly on the lane, even if it's very oily. We're talking about conditions in which an old-fashioned ball, with a mere reactive cover, would hydroplane on the lane dressing. Proactive gets grip. This increases the hook potential and evens the arc of a ball's path. The little tiny textures also lessen the wear and tear on the ball. Can you hear the bickering? "Lasts longer!" "Hooks better!" "Lasts longer!" "Hooks better!"

CERAMIC CORES

It has been found that a ball's hitting power can be enhanced by placing at its center a ceramic core. Whereas other materials at the core of the ball will absorb energy from the pins on contact, the ceramic core reabsorbs nothing, so all of the energy is transferred from the ball to the pins.

The ceramics used in bowling balls is called *fired ceramics*. Whereas millable or alloy ceramics absorb energy, fired ceramics repel it, sending all of the power into the pins and making them fly. The bottom line is, a ball with a ceramic core hits harder. Two manufacturers who use fired ceramic cores in their bowling balls are Columbia 300 and Track.

SPECIAL NOTE ON CLEANING NEW FANGLED BALLS

The new super, ultradynamic state-of-the-art nuclear-powered bowling balls can eat up $300 or more worth of lettuce and, when they first went on the market, had a reputation for losing their effectiveness after about six months of steady use.

The reason was simple: The tacky surface on resin balls attracted dirt and crud and wax. Proactive balls can have their microscopic nooks and crannies filled up with various yucky substances on the lane. It was then discovered that the bowling balls could have their life span extended with proper cleaning.

Proactive and reactive balls should be washed once every twelve to fifteen games, which amounts to about once a month for the weekly bowler. (Failure to wash the ball regularly will cause dirt and lane oil to be absorbed right into the shell of the bowling ball, causing permanent damage.) All balls should be washed, but it's particularly important with balls of this type.

Some easy-to-follow instructions for cleaning your ball:

1. Tape the holes shut with electric tape.
2. Fill a large bowl with hot water. Add grease-cutting detergent. Do *not* use a floor cleaner that contains wax, as this will make your problems worse rather than better.
3. Wash the ball with a lint-free cloth. Remember to give some extra elbow grease to the tracking area of your ball, the area where it most frequently comes into contact with the lane.

Here are some commercial bowling-ball cleaners—as well as solvents and other chemicals—that are great for cleaning your ball, and a list of cleaners that are *not* to be used. Do not get the two lists confused or your bowling ball will soon resemble a meteorite.

GOOD Cleaners

- Clean Shot—Earth Clean Systems
- Maz's Ball Klean—David Mahaz
- Oil B Gone—Pro-Tech Industrial Chemical
- Perfect Grip—Bowling Concepts
- Pro Grip—DBA Products
- Protrac 19—Richardson International Corp.
- Reacta Clean—High Score Products
- Reese Brothers Ball Clean
- Strike It Clean—Bowl Products, Inc.
- U-Clean U-Score—High Score Products
- Clean Shot Reactive Ball Cleaner—Earth Clean Systems
- Pro-Grip Reactive Ball Cleaner—DBA Products
- Squeeky Clean—The Wax Shop
- Bowling Ball Cleaner—Forrest Enterprises, Inc.

BAD Cleaners

- Strike Power—Veterans Products
- SS-25
- Varsol
- Dull It—INX Corp.

GOOD Solvents and Chemicals

- Rubbing alcohol (isopropyl)
- Simple Green
- Windex
- Armor All

BAD Solvents and Chemicals

- Other alcohols (i.e., denatured ethyl alcohol)
- Acetone (nail-polish remover)
- Kerosene, gasoline, and other fuels
- Ethers, esters, and ketone (MEK)
- Most commercial solvents (xylene, lacquer thinner, mineral spirits, chloroform, methyl hydrate)

Be aware that, even if washed properly and regularly, your reactive ball will not remain nuclear-powered forever. The natural wear of bowling on the ball will decrease the shell's tackiness or smooth out the microscopic texturing—just as a tremendous number of miles will inevitably cause a car's tire to become bald.

HAVING THE HOLES DRILLED

So you bought your ball. There's one problem, though: no holes. Don't pull out the drill. These things must be done very delicately.

See a pro. The configuration in which you get your finger holes drilled is called your *grip*.

According to John Illiano, who handles the drill in the pro shop at Mark Lanes in Brooklyn, there are three kinds of grips, all three of which allow full insertion of the thumb:

1. the conventional fit, which allows the middle and ring fingers to be inserted two-thirds of the way;
2. the semi-fingertip fit, used most often by advanced bowlers, which allows your middle two fingers to go halfway in;
3. and the fingertip grip, used almost exclusively by advanced bowlers, which allows insertion of the fingers to the first knuckle.

You want the conventional grip. It provides a firmer finger hold, allowing you greater control over your release point. Pro bowlers have ungodly strong hands, with wrists like oak, so a lesser insertion for their fingers gives them extra "touch." You and I, we would drop the ball way early. Ninety-nine out of 100 house balls have the conventional grip.

The first thing John does in preparation for drilling your ball is measure your fingers. Until recently, John had a mock bowling ball with holes of many different sizes, and he used it to determine which hole best matched each bowler's fingers. But that ball broke, so John now has to use a tape measure. It's old-fashioned, but it works.

Before drilling into your ball, John determines the appropriate *pitch* you want in your finger holes. The pitch is the amount of deviation of the axis of a hole away from or toward the geometric center of the ball. If you don't know what pitch you want—and only very serious bowlers do—John will have you try balls that have been drilled at various pitches to determine which is most comfortable for you.

Some bowling balls come with what is called topweight. Since the drilling of the holes is bound to make the ball heavier on one side than on the other, the topweight is put in to maintain the balance.

The holes are drilled in the heavier side, and after the holes are made both sides weigh the same.

What does the modern pro use to drill a bowling ball? Well, since it was recently discovered that most drills are round, yet fingers are oval, the American Machine and Foundry's vaccu-jig drilling machine has become a pro-shop favorite. The vaccu-jig can drill ovals into the bowling ball, so that your grip can be more comfortable than ever.

SHOES

There are two reasons for wearing bowling shoes when you bowl. Dress shoes, with leather or hard rubber soles, can mark and damage the approach area. They would also provide lousy footing on the slippery boards of the approach area.

Sneakers are no good either, not because they'll damage the wood but because they have no slide. The proper bowling delivery necessitates a sliding lead foot toward the foul line. Try that in sneakers and you foul with your nose.

If you were looking for some plain black bowling shoes, fuhgeddaboudit! Bowling shoes come in two styles: colorful and brightly colorful. (Actually, that's not true. You can get plain white or plain black shoes—if you feel the need to look dignified and bowl at the same time, that is.)

Bowling shoes are designed so that you don't slip and slide around when you're walking around the bowling center, yet you can slide comfortably to the foul line. The amount of friction has to be just right. The best bowling shoes have rubber soles, except at the toe, which is made of soft leather. It is on this area that you slide at the end of the delivery. House shoes have leather under both the right and the left toes to accommodate both right- and left-handed bowlers.

When you buy your own shoes—available at all better sporting-goods stores—you may elect to get a pair that is specifically built for righties or lefties. The right-handed shoes have the soft leather sole only on the left shoe, while the right shoe has an all-rubber sole. This ensures better footing during the approach yet provides the same amount of slide at the finish.

Sometimes new bowling shoes don't have the desired amount of slide. The left shoe for right-handed bowlers has to slide to within one-zillionth of an inch of the foul line without ever crossing it, and for this the shoe must slide perfectly. The best way to get the shoes to slide properly is to use them. Normal wear will decrease the friction on brand-new shoes. If you need to fix the problem *right now*, because you're in a tournament or something like that, you can sand the sharp edge of the shoes' heels so that they are rounded. If more emergency treatment is needed, there are products such as Easy-Glide, which can be put on the bottom of your shoes to increase their slide.

Be very, very careful, however, about putting substances on the bottoms of your bowling shoes. You can easily create a dangerous situation for yourself. If having too much glide were a desirable thing in bowling, this game would be played on ice.

OTHER EQUIPMENT

In addition to a bowling ball and a pair of shoes of your own, there's lots of other equipment that will improve your game and make you look both savvy and snappy while you're bowling.

One of the neatest thingamajigs are finger-hole inserts, which are usually made of something smooth, like plastic, to lessen the abrasiveness of the inside of some bowling balls, thus preventing blisters. A new item designed for the thumbhole is the *Thumbillow*. Here's something that can help both your control and your power, and it costs only about five bucks.

One reason bowlers miss their mark is that they bowl with a ball that has an ill-fitting thumbhole. Even if your ball has been perfectly custom-drilled, your thumb changes size all the time. It can change size because of weight gain or loss over the long term, but it can also expand and shrink over the course of a night's bowling because of heat, exertion, and wear. Thus the Thumbillow, which is a smooth, padded cushion that fits inside the thumbhole, on the fingernail side. It gives and takes so that your thumb always fits perfectly in the hole, and you can get the best possible delivery with each roll.

If the thumbhole in your ball is too loose, you can expect a number of negative manifestations in your delivery:

1. Early release with no lift
2. Short backswing with a bent elbow
3. A short pushaway

As a result, the ball will skid rather than roll and strike the pins with diminished power.

On the other hand, if the thumbhole is too tight—a more common problem, since we tend to gain weight more than we lose it, and our thumbs are more apt to swell than shrink as an evening of bowling goes along—there are also a number of ill effects:

1. Your thumb may become sore, causing you to reduce your power in an attempt to stop further irritation.
2. Your thumb will remain in the hole after the intended release point, causing you to loft the ball and lose accuracy.
3. You will bend your elbow to reduce the pressure on your thumb, and then muscle the ball in an attempt to compensate for lost energy.

Obviously, the Thumbillow can't make the thumbhole larger; only a pro shop can do that. But the Thumbillow is so thin that it doesn't make the hole any tighter, and, because it is a smooth and soft surface, it definitely lessens the irritation that a too-small thumbhole can cause. And some say the additional comfort it provides makes the ball feel lighter during delivery.

WRIST PROTECTOR

A wrist protector is worn on the bowling wrist to keep it steady during the delivery. This is excellent for folks with unstable wrists that might collapse at a key moment, causing the ball to be dropped, or, in severe cases, cause a backup ball—one that hooks in the opposite direction. Expert bowlers wear them, too. Some of the pros' wrist protectors look as if they were straight out of *The Jetsons*, with control knobs that supposedly adjust the size of the hook.

CHAPTER 6

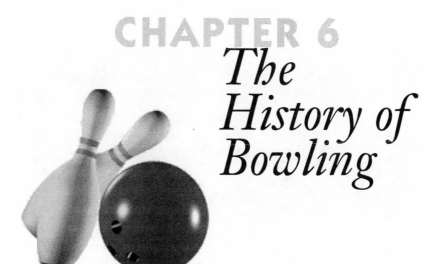

The History of Bowling

TODAY, BOWLING IS enjoyed by more than 100 million people in more than 100 countries. But where did it all start? Bowling isn't like basketball or American football. We cannot identify the inventor. We can't place the first game. However, it's safe to say that bowling was around long before chariot racing. The Flintstones bowl, and that may be the only thing about cavemen that the cartoonists got right.

In the 1930s, a ball and nine marble pins were found in an Egyptian tomb by the British anthropologist Sir Flinders Petrie. The bowling set was buried sometime around 5200 B.C.—although from the size and shape of the items it seems the rank and file along the Nile played a predecessor of candlepin bowling (a form of the game that we'll be discussing in Chapter 7). In fourth-century Germany, according to the historian William Pehle, men rolled a ball at a single pin, called a *heathen*. Knocking down the heathen was supposed to be a demonstration of religious faith.

Bowling retained its mystical qualities throughout the Dark Ages, when men bowled at multiple pins to predict their future. A strike meant the bowler would remain virtuous. Leaving too many pins

Throughout history, the act of using a small handheld ball to either bowl at other small balls (lawn bowling and bocce) or at pins has been a popular leisure-time sport. Here, a game of skittles is being played in 1588 by the great English admiral Sir Francis Drake. In the background, the Spanish Armada approaches in the English Channel.

standing forecasted the road to ruin. Today, there are many pro bowlers (and their wives) who still believe this to be true.

Bowling took different forms as it spread across Europe. It became *bocce* in Italy around the year A.D. 1100, and *lawn bowling* in England around the same time. The wooden alley made its debut 100 years later, in a version of the game played in Holland, Switzerland, and Germany in which nine pins, arranged in three rows of three, were set up on an alley that consisted of a single plank of wood one to one and a half feet wide. In Germany, the game was known as *kegling*, and the bowlers as *keglers*. In some German neighborhoods in the United States, these terms are still used.

All bowling at pins was done outdoors in England for the first 300 years the game was played there, hence the name lawn bowling. The first indoor bowling alley recorded for posterity was used in 1455 by an imaginative nobleman, and that was thirty-seven years before Christopher Columbus discovered that the earth was shaped like a bowling ball.

Modern tenpin bowling is extremely popular in Great Britain today, as are many similar games that were English offshoots over the years—games such as *skittles*, *half-bowls* and *ninepins*.

But, believe it or not, bowling was once banned in England by King Edward III. It was in the 1330s and the people, he found, were a little too fond of bowling. They weren't spending what His Royal Highness thought to be adequate hours practicing their archery skills. Edward was particularly worried about the soldiers in his army, and rightfully so, as they would soon need those skills in the upcoming Hundred Years' War.

It took a while, but bowling reworked its way back into English life. By the time of Henry VIII, bowling was again the rage in merry ol' England. On October 15, 1520, Henry VIII ordered bowling lanes to be built at Whitehall in London. During the sixteenth century, Sir Francis Drake himself insisted on finishing up his final frame before taking action against the Spanish Armada, which was attacking from the English Channel.

Bowling was first played in America in 1626, on Manhattan Island—the very same island upon which the author, 350 years later, bowled a 201 with a five-strike finish. The first Manhattan bowlers were Dutch settlers, who bowled a ninepin game. They built an outdoor bowling facility along lower Broadway in an area that is known to this day as Bowling Green.

The Pilgrims throwing a small ball at small pins in the early 1600s. This artwork is exhibited at the Plymouth Plantation, Plymouth, Massachusetts.

The History of Bowling

The sport spread northward into what is now Westchester County, in upstate New York, and then into Connecticut. Washington Irving was a bowler, and featured bowling in his 1820 story *Rip Van Winkle*. In fact, it was the sound of "crashing nine pins" that awoke Van Winkle from his time-bending snooze.

The modern tenpin game was first played to get past a poorly worded law. It was 1842, and once again bowling was at the center of a controversy. So addictive was this marvelous sport that it was feared it would seduce the public into malingering. Professional matches attracted much gambling, and rigged matches sometimes led to violence. The Connecticut state legislature specifically banned ninepin bowling. Smart promoters, when they read the wording of the new law, burst into wide grins. They simply added a tenth pin, arranged them in the current triangle configuration, and stayed in business. Weary lawmakers conceded their defeat—and bowling went on.

By the late nineteenth century, bowling was being played throughout the U.S. Northeast and Midwest, with New York and Chicago being hubs of activity. But the size and weight of the pins, balls, and lanes varied from region to region.

On September 9, 1895, the restaurateur Joe Thum gathered representatives from various bowling clubs around the country to meet at Beethoven Hall in New York City. There, the assembled reps formed the American Bowling Congress (ABC), and the rules of bowling were standardized for the first time. Specifications for the size and weight of the ball, the pins and the alleys were all put into place. Balls were to be between six and sixteen pounds. The alley had to be forty-two inches wide and sixty feet long. There were to be ten frames in a game, with each frame consisting of two balls thrown at the pins, unless all of the pins are knocked down with the first ball for a strike. A bonus ball or two was awarded to those who scored a spare or a strike in the final frame. Scoring was based on the number of pins knocked down, with the maximum score being 300. The ABC held its first tournament for professional and amateur bowlers in 1901.

Up until the turn of the century, bowling balls were made out of very hard wood, with lignum vitae being the favorite. It wasn't until 1905 that the first rubber bowling ball was manufactured. It was called the Evertrue. The Brunswick Corporation, a name that's still very big in the world of bowling, began manufacturing balls in 1914. It's first model was called the Mineralite Ball. The company bragged of its new ball's "mysterious rubber compound."

In those days, your average bowling alley was in the cellar of a saloon, and there was probably only one lane, with one pin boy returning the ball to the bowler, putting the pins back up, and clearing felled pins out of the way for spare attempts. Some members of the upper class had a bowling alley in their homes. There was no such thing as a bowling center with many lanes side by side.

The Women's International Bowling Congress was formed, in St. Louis, Missouri, in 1916—and began holding tournaments for the best lady bowlers the following year—but it wasn't until the Great Depression that bowling changed its look to become more appealing to women. The dimness of the tavern basement was replaced with a brighter, more colorful decor. Bowlers now got to wear flashy shoes, and shirts that looked great with one's name embroidered on the breast. The bowling alley was still often attached to a bar, but now, more often than not, it was above ground, and there were several

This is what most bowlers saw at the alleys until 1953. Even the most experienced and dedicated pin boys couldn't set up pins exactly the same way every time, even though pin spots were used to guide them. When they finished setting the ten pins they would jump up to the high bench in back of the pits.

lanes, so that bowling parties could be held and bowling leagues could be formed.

Not long afterward, in 1936, the engineer Fred Schmidt took a bicycle chain, flower pots, and various machine parts and made the first automatic pinspotter. Schmidt's invention came to the attention of Morehead Patterson, the chairman of the board of the American Machine and Foundry Company (AMF) and, in 1946, the modern mechanical pinspotter made its debut in Buffalo, New York, for that year's American Bowling Congress Tournament. Until then, AMF had made equipment for bakery, tobacco, and apparel businesses.

It was another five years before the machines were coming off the assembly line regularly, but by that time they were selling as fast as they could be made. There was a bowling boom in the early 1950s, with one or more bowling alleys guaranteed to be "opening up near you."

Today, most bowling centers are smoke free, with designated smoking areas— usually the bar. But back in the late 1950s, when this picture was taken, it was rare that an establishment—such as the White Oak Lanes in Silver Springs, Maryland—would brag of their smoke-free air.

At the same time, television was entering American homes by the millions, and bowling turned out to be perfect for the boob tube. Pro bowlers became full-fledged TV stars and, consequently, everybody else bowled more than ever. The Professional Bowlers Association bowed in 1958 as a sanctioning body for televised tournaments, and the *Pro Bowlers Tour* , became a staple on TV for the next forty years. In 1959, the Professional Women Bowlers Association held its first tournament. That organization has since simplified its name to the Ladies Pro Bowlers' Tour.

TV SHOWS

The first network coverage of bowling was *Bowling Headliners*, which ran from December 26, 1948, until October 30, 1949, on ABC, and then from November 13, 1949, until April 9, 1950, on the Dumont network. It was a half-hour series that was hosted by Jimmy Powers in its ABC incarnation and by Al Cirillo when it was on Dumont.

There was another show called *Bowling Stars*, which featured head-to-head matches. It also ran on two different networks, for a short stint on ABC during 1957 with "Whispering" Joe Wilson as the host, and during the 1960–61 season on NBC with Bud Palmer behind the mike. Whispering Joe got his name because he spoke in a whisper so as not to disturb the bowlers.

National Bowling Champions ran on NBC during the 1956–57 season. The late-night show was also hosted by Whispering Joe.

Make That Spare ran from October 15, 1960, to September 11, 1964, on ABC, with Johnny Johnston as the host, except during the 1960–61 season, when Win Elliot hosted.

On January 6, 1962, ABC started broadcasting the finals of the weekly Pro Bowlers Tour tournaments, and that show—*Pro Bowlers' Tour*—ran for thirty-five years, with Chris Schenkel as the host from start to finish.

Sitting beside Schenkel doing the color commentary were Jack Buck (1962–64), Billy Welu (1964–74), and Nelson Burton, Jr. (1975–97).

In 1982, the Young American Bowling Alliance formed to promote and regulate bowling for youngsters, as well as high-school and college-aged bowlers.

In 1988, bowling became a demonstration sport in the Summer Olympics—and there are hopes that it will one day be a medal sport.

Not all has been rosy for bowling over the last few years. In 1997, the *Pro Bowlers' Tour* was canceled by ABC, marking the first time since 1961 that the tournament finals were not broadcast on network television.

In 1998, pro bowling could be found only on cable's ESPN. After only one year off network television, the *Pro Bowlers' Tour* signed a new contract with CBS. The PBA promises that the new telecasts will modernize the game and bring it into the twenty-first century.

FIRST OUTDOOR EVENT

The PBA Tour took a major step toward shucking its old image in favor of something more modern and crowd-pleasing on May 1, 1999, when it held its first event outdoors.

The opening rounds of the Long Island Open were held at the Coram Country Lanes in Coram, New York. The final round, the TV round, was renamed the New York City Bowling Experience, and two lanes were put up in the Big Apple's Bryant Park. The park is located between Fifth and Sixth Avenues, and between Forty-first and Forty-second Streets, directly behind the New York Public Library, the one with the lions out front.

The lanes were built in the Brunswick Corporation's factory and shipped to Bryant Park, where they were constructed by a crew headed by Mike Arkins. In case of rain, a tent would have been erected over the lanes to protect them, but, luckily for everyone, it turned out to be a beautiful spring day—sixty-seven degrees, thirteen-miles-per-hour winds, not a cloud in the sky.

When the official bowling began, the lanes were measured at 95° F because of the intense sun. That's a solid twenty degrees hotter than they ever get during an indoor tournament. The heat was making the oil run farther down the lanes than usual, creating conditions that were unprecedented.

Of four bowlers who got to bowl on TV, the first seed was twenty-nine-year-old Mark "Wasabi" Mosayebi, a seven-year pro who bowled a perfect game in the early rounds. A Sheetrock finisher from Charlotte, North Carolina, this was his first No. 1 seed.

The three bowlers who would compete in the "shootout round" were the second seed, left-handed John Mazza, of Bay City, Michigan, who was also enjoying his best-ever finish after the preliminary rounds; third seed Eric Forkel of Chatsworth, California, an eleven-year tour veteran who chewed gum and wore sunglasses during the event; and Rudy "Revs" Kasimakis, who was bowling on TV for the second consecutive week.

Rudy had trouble reining in his big hook under the unpredictable lane conditions and bowled a 200 during the shootout round. This was respectable but not nearly good enough to win. Mazza had a 236, but even that wasn't close to the 267 bowled by the gum-chewing and shades-wearing Forkel, whose smooth delivery and compact hook seemed perfectly suited to the day. The final match was closer, with Forkel defeating Mosayebi 243–231. Mosayebi had a chance to win it right up until the final frame, when he was stymied by a Six-Seven-Ten split. To compound his disaster he threw his second shot into the channel. Forkel won the tourney and the $17,000 in first-place prize money.

And so the first outdoor event in PBA history was over. Though the unusual venue made bowling feel brand-new for a moment, the emotions of the competitors were as old as pro bowling itself. Forkel was elated over his winnings. Mosayebi was in tears because he still had to keep his day job.

All because of the way the pins fell.

How a PBA Tournament Works

The bowlers, who are collectively known as the *field*, bowl eighteen games apiece in three six-game rounds. The first two rounds are held on Wednesday and the third on Thursday. The top-twenty-four bowlers with the highest total score after eighteen games remain. The rest can go home. The remaining group then bowls another twenty-four games, this time in three eight-game sets—the first on Thursday night, the second on Friday afternoon, and the third on Friday night.

During the years that ABC broadcast the finals of the tournaments on TV, the top-five bowlers would bowl on Saturday in individual one-on-one one-game matches, held in a stepladder fashion. That is, the bowler with the fifth-best total score after forty-two games would bowl against the bowler with the fourth-best score. The winner of that one-game match would bowl against the bowler with the third-best cumulative score, and so on. The top-scoring bowler of the week had to bowl only one game in order to win the tournament.

That format has been revised by CBS, which is more concerned about fitting the entire process into a one-hour time slot. Only the top-four bowlers now make it onto TV. Those seeded two, three, and four have a one-game roll-off. The bowler with the best game then bowls one-on-one against the No. 1 seeded bowler for all the marbles.

CHAPTER 7

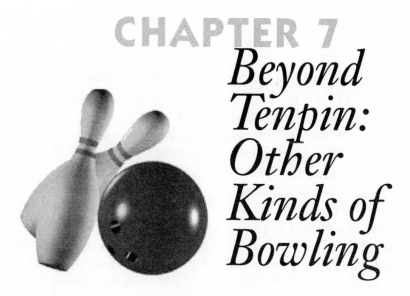

Beyond Tenpin: Other Kinds of Bowling

SINCE BOWLING IS so old—indeed prehistoric—it is to be expected that its history is not a straight line but, rather, a tree with branches. Over the years, variations of the game have become popular in their own right.

Here is a brief look at several different types of bowling that are worth exploring.

DUCKPINS

Duckpin bowling was invented in 1900 by Frank Van Sant, the manager of Diamond Alleys on Howard Street in Baltimore, Maryland, and John Dettmar, a local woodturner.

Baseball fans will be interested to know that the owners of the bowling alley were John McGraw and Uncle Wilbert Robinson, both of whom are now members of the Baseball Hall of Fame. McGraw was the longtime manager of the New York Giants, while Robinson skippered the Brooklyn Dodgers.

Because human pinsetters were a lot more flexible than the mechanical kind, bowlers could play strange, sometimes self-invented games if they wanted to. Games were played using only the One, Seven, and Ten pins. These contests were known as *cocked-hat* games. Another game called *five back* used only the back row and the Five Pin. For these games, the alley used balls that were six inches in diameter. When someone suggested that an interesting game might develop if an old set of ten pins were whittled down to a smaller size so that all ten could be used with a smaller ball, Van Sant set Dettmar to the task and the first duckpins were made.

Apart from the size of the ball and the pins, the game was played exactly like tenpin bowling—and scored the same way as well. It's still played this way today. The game earned its name when Robinson and McGraw commented that the flying pins looked like a "flock of ducks." *Baltimore Sun* sportswriter Bill Clarke overheard the remark, printed it, and the name stuck.

During the next four years, the game spread to nearby Washington, D.C., and leagues were formed. Intercity competitions were established. The Washington City Duckpin Association held its first meeting in 1910.

Until 1927, duckpins was confined mostly to Baltimore and Washington, but word spread. That year, a group of duckpin bowlers, led by George Isemann of Washington, D.C., and Frank Zihlman, a Republican congressman from Cumberland, Maryland, organized the National Duckpin Bowling Congress (NDBC). Congressman Zihlman was named its first president, and Isemann its first executive secretary.

With the sport now being played from Boston to Atlanta, Isemann worked to bring standardization to the game. Within a few years, and with the help of several manufacturers, duckpins were standardized. Uniform lane conditions and regulation size and weight of balls followed. The balls were to be five inches in diameter and weigh no more than three pounds twelve ounces.

The first annual National Tournament was held in 1928 at the Recreation Alleys in Baltimore. There were 201 singles, 162 doubles, and 126 team entries in that tournament. By 1967, the fortieth year of the NDBC, the National Tournament had grown to include 1,444

Duckpin World Records

Adult

Men's High Game: 279, Pete Signore, Jr., March 5, 1992, T-Bowl Lanes, Newington, Connecticut.

Women's High Game: 265, Carole Gittings, May 6, 1973, Fair Lanes Timonium, Timonium, Maryland.

Men's High Three-Game Set: 655, Jeff Pyles, April 24, 1978, Glenmont Bowl, Wheaton, Maryland.

Women's High Three-Game Set: 586, Diane Sicca, June 16, 1988, Suitland Bowl, Suitland, Maryland.

Men's High Season Average: 164.47, Jeff Pyles, 1982–83, Wheaton Triangle, Wheaton, Maryland.

Women's High Season Average: 151.98, Diane Sicca, 1986–87, Suitland Bowl, Suitland, Maryland.

Youth

Boy's High Game: 247, Jim Kaufmann, March 13, 1989, Cheshire, Connecticut.

Girl's High Game: 262, Amy Bisson, March 4, 1995, Newington, Connecticut.

Boy's High Three-Game Set: 583, Dave Wander, March 6, 1993, Reiserstown, Maryland.

Girl's High Three-Game Set: 567, Amy Bisson, October 30, 1994, Newington, Connecticut.

Boy's High Season Average: 149, Chuck King, 1988–89, Baltimore, Maryland; 149, Paul Weaver, 1996–97, Richmond, Virginia.

Girl's High Season Average: 144, Amy Bisson, 1993–94, Newington, Connecticut.

teams, 897 doubles, and 1,701 singles entries. During the 1966–67 season, the 40th year of sanctioned duckpin bowling, nearly 300,000 bowlers and 50,000 teams were sanctioned by the NDBC.

The sport peaked in popularity during the 1960s, and the number of bowlers who aim at the flock of ducks gets smaller each year. Predictably, the Washington/Baltimore area once again became the focal point of the sport during the latter part of the twentieth century.

CANDLEPIN BOWLING

Candlepin bowling was invented in Worcester, Massachusetts, in 1890 by Justin P. White, a billiard-room owner, and John J. Monsey, a billiard expert. Monsey thought that the ball and the pins in regular tenpin bowling were too large and heavy. By making the pins and the balls smaller and lighter, he figured, the game could be played by more people.

The first candlepin was eleven inches high and was tapered to an inch in diameter at either end. The ball was made of wood, weighed about two pounds, and was four and a half inches in diameter. Today, the official maximum weight of the ball is two pounds seven ounces. Balls one or two ounces lighter than that are most popular. The ball is gripped with the fingers and thumb, and held firmly, away from the palm of the hand. Looking down at those tapered pins is like looking at ten candles atop a wooden birthday cake. Naming the game was easy. The lanes are the same as those for the tenpin alleys.

The pins are set up just as they would be for a regulation tenpin game, but since they are so slender the space between the pins has increased. Blend into the mix the fact that the ball is much smaller and you'll see that it's a very different game. To compensate for the

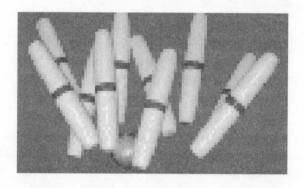

Definitions of Candlepin Terms

barn door
: Any favorable wood (fallen pins) directly in front of the key pin(s).

cleanup
: Get all remaining pins with the third ball, the cleanup ball.

dead wood
: Sometimes referred to as just "wood." Fallen pins are not swept away, as in standard tenpin bowling, and can be used to knock down additional pins with subsequent two balls.

fair zone
: Portion of the lane between the foul line and the lob line.

lob
: To toss the ball over the lob line, which is ten feet beyond the foul line. A lob is scored as a foul, and the bowler receives no points for that frame, regardless of which of the three balls the foul was committed with.

punch out
: Down a pin or pins from the middle of a leave only.

puzzle
: Where wood is an obstruction or is difficult to figure out.

sweeper
: Wood that downs the remaining pins.

additional difficulty in knocking down the candlepins, bowlers are allowed three rolls instead of two, and the fallen pin—the dead wood, as it is called—instead of being swept away after every shot, remains where it is and can be used to knock down the remaining pins.

As was true of all forms of bowling, candlepin bowling was dependent on pinsetters until automatic machines were introduced. When automatic pinsetters were first made, almost as many candlepin-setters were made as those designed for regular pins. Over the years, however, the production of automatic candlepin pinsetters has decreased to practically nil, and most candlepin alleys have very old machines.

Still, candlepins spread throughout New England and the Canadian Atlantic seaboard, replacing the skittle alleys, where larger pins and disks rather than balls were used. Today, candlepins is played everywhere from Los Angeles to Germany.

Because of the size of the balls, the candlepin lanes in many bowling centers, where both candlepin and traditional bowling are available, are transformed into day-care centers while parents bowl in their leagues.

FIVEPIN BOWLING

Fivepin bowling may be the only purely Canadian sport left. The Canadians have invented many sports, hockey being the most notable. All but one have become international. If you want to bowl the fivepin game, you had better be in Canada, or you're out of luck.

The game was first developed in 1908 by Thomas F. Ryan, the proprietor of the Bowladrome, in Canada. The major complaints about tenpin bowling at the time were that the ball was too heavy and the pins took too long to be set up by the pinsetters.

Ryan made two changes: He made the ball smaller and lighter, and he changed the number of pins from ten to five. Another thing he noticed was that pinsetters were slowed down by the size of the pins, so he made them smaller as well. The first Five Pin, a regular Ten Pin that had been whittled down, was made in Ryan's father's workshop. Since candlepin bowling already existed, Ryan borrowed that ball for his game.

Like candlepin bowling, fivepin bowlers get three rolls in each frame. Unlike candlepin bowling, however, the lane is swept between rolls to remove the fallen pins. The scoring is very similar to tenpin scoring, except that you receive a different number of points depending on which pins you knock down. Knocking over the headpin earns you five points. The two pins flanking the headpin score three points apiece, while the back-corner pins score two points apiece. Though there are only five pins, fifteen points can be scored by knocking them all down.

Strikes (knocking down all five pins with the first ball), and spares, (knocking down all of the pins with the first two balls), earn bonus points—equivalent to those in tenpin bowling. For a strike, you can add on the total of your next two balls, and for a spare you add on the score of your next ball.

The maximum possible score in a game is 450, which is a real challenge to achieve. Most bowlers are extremely happy to get a 300 game, and anyone with an average of more than 250 is considered a top-caliber bowler.

BUMPERS

Sometimes the simplest ideas are most effective. Such is the case with bumpers. For years, kids had to be a certain age before they had the combination of strength and coordination required to roll an eight-pound bowling ball all the way down a lane without sending it into the channel.

Bumpers are little rubber curbs that don't interfere with normal bowling when they are snapped down, but when they are snapped up they become walls that run up and down the entire length of the lane on either side, preventing the ball from going into the gutter. Now any kid who can roll the ball with two hands can knock down pins.

Sometimes the balls bounce off the bumpers four or five times before they get there, but they do get there, and the kids squeal with delight and jump up and down with joy when the pins fall. By the time most children are old enough to bowl without the bumpers, they're hooked on the game. After all, knocking down the pins is the fun part, so what if bowling has made it a little easier for the five-to-ten crowd?

GLOW BOWLING

Of course, to each his own, but the recent movement to make bowling more popular by making it darker and louder escapes me. Well, it doesn't escape me, it just doesn't have anything to do with me.

These changes are making the local bowling alley a hot venue for dates.

What is glow bowling? Or disco bowling, or galactic bowling—or whatever it is they call it at your local bowling center?

Well, envision this: Fog machines pump an eerie cloud of steam throughout the bowling center. The house lights go out and 378 feet of crystallite rope lighting flows down the lanes. As the music begins, high-powered halogen-effect lights combine with lasers to make the place come alive! Not just a couple of lights, not just a couple of dozen, but enough to rival any nightclub.

The sound system cranks out your favorite dance music. A video-display system plays music videos. The building pulsates from sub-woofers, known as Earthquakes. An Intelligent Lighting effects system thrills the senses. Six new theatrical lights shine different colors and patterns all over the walls and ceiling. With more than forty different effects, colors, patterns, speeds—you name it, it's got it—it looks awesome!

Of course, if you take your bowling seriously, be aware that the music can be numbing to the senses, and with all the dancing lights it can be difficult, if not impossible, to see the arrows and dots on the lanes.

Records and Milestones

PERFECT 900 SERIES

The first bowler to roll an American Bowling Congress perfect 900 series—thirty-six rolls, thirty-six strikes—was twenty-six-year-old University of Nebraska sophomore Jeremy Sonnenfeld, who did it during tournament play at Sun Valley Lanes in Lincoln, Nebraska, on February 2, 1997.

Sonnenfeld, who's from Sioux Falls, South Dakota, earned his NOBODY'S PERFECT, EXCEPT ME T-shirt across six lanes in the middle squad of the Junior Husker Tournament. The business major, and a collegiate all-American as a freshman, had rolled four previous 300 games. He had bowled three previous 800-plus three-games series, with his previous personal best being an 826, which he scored on December 3, 1994. The previous record three-game series score, as recognized by the American Bowling Congress, was 899 (that's knocking down everything but a tenth-frame tenpin in one of the three games).

Two other bowlers had rolled three consecutive 300 games—Troy Ockerman of Owosso, Michigan, on December 18, 1993, and Norm Duke of North Brunswick, New Jersey, who did it on April 10, 1996—but those feats did not count as a perfect three-game series because the consecutive perfect games were rolled in separate squads during tournament play.

On November 9, 1998, in the Variety Club Midwest Challenge League at Classic Lanes in Greenfield, Wisconsin, Tony Roventini became the second bowler to roll an American Bowling Congress–approved 900 series.

Roventini—a twenty-eight-year-old model engineer for a construction, agricultural, and recreational equipment manufacturer—brought his lifetime total of perfect games to eighteen. He had six 800-plus series before this, with 857 being his previous personal best. He bowled his perfect series as the leadoff bowler for his Pro World team on Lanes 3 and 4 of the sixteen-lane alley just outside Milwaukee.

300 GAMES ON TV

Here's a sad story. The 1999 PBA Tour event known as the Chattanooga Open, held at the Holiday Bowl in Chattanooga, Tennessee, was to be televised on ESPN on a tape-delay basis. During the finals of the tournament, cameras were rolling. And so was Steve Jaros. On February 13, 1999, Jaros, of Bolingbrook, Illinois, rolled a perfect game in the second rung of the stepladder finals, bowling against Ricky Ward—and became the thirteenth bowler to roll a perfect game on TV.

Or, did he?

Just as Jaros was being mobbed and the place was going nuts, there was a guy out in the TV production truck who was sweating bullets. The tape hadn't come out, and no backup had been made. So the match never aired. ESPN, good guys that they are, paid Jaros the $10,000 bonus for bowling a perfect game on TV despite the foul-up.

And so, until someone else comes along who can put twelve strikes together on TV, the number of televised perfect games remains at twelve, with the most recent being that of Parker Bohn III, who did it in Reno, Nevada, on May 9, 1998. His opponent was Chris Sand, who bowled a 246 and lost by fifty-four pins.

The eleventh perfect game belonged to Steve Hoskins, who did it in the semis of the PBA Ebonite Challenge at Marcel's Olympic Bowl in Rochester, New York, on October 16, 1997.

Here are the official twelve bowlers who have bowled perfect 300 games on television:

1. Jack Biondolillo, Akron, Ohio, April 1, 1967.

2. John Guenther, San Jose, California, February 1, 1969.

3. Jim Stefanich, Alameda, California, January 5, 1974.

4. Pete McCordic, Torrance, California, January 31, 1987.

5. Bob Benoit, Grand Prairie, Texas, January 23, 1988. (First 300 game in a title match.)

6. Mike Aulby, Wichita, Kansas, July 31, 1993.

7. Johnny Petraglia, Toledo, Ohio, March 5, 1994.

8. Butch Soper, Reno, Nevada, July 12, 1994.

9. C. K. Moore, Austin, Texas, February 2, 1996.

10. Bob Learn, Jr., Erie, Pennsylvania, April 6, 1996.

11. Steve Hoskins, Rochester, New York, October 15, 1997.

12. Parker Bohn III, Reno, Nevada, May 9, 1998.

YOUNGEST 300 SHOOTER

The youngest bowler to roll a perfect game is Josey LaRocco. When he shot his gem on Valentine's Day 1999, in Louisville, Kentucky, LaRocco was ten years, six months, and twenty-seven days old.

LaRocco had earlier told his mother, Gail, that he was going to break the record for the youngest bowler to achieve perfection. He bowled his perfect game in his first game of his Saturday morning Bantam and Prep league at AMF Derby Lanes. He used a twelve-pound ball. He had been bowling for only one year when he, for ten frames anyway, stopped making mistakes.

The previous record belonged to Scott Owsley of Fontana, California, who was ten years, nine months, and six days old when he put together twelve straight strikes on March 26, 1994.

Third place belongs to Sean Wyandt of Sinking Springs, Pennsylvania, who rolled a 300 on June 5, 1994, at the age of ten years, eleven months, and twenty-one days.

OLDEST 300 BOWLERS

The oldest man to bowl a perfect game is Joe Norris of San Diego, California, who rolled his on December 14, 1994, at the age of eighty-six years, ten months, and six days. The oldest woman is Myrt Kressin of Bremerton, Washington, who rolled twelve straight on February 8, 1997, at the age of seventy-one years, five months, and seven days.

HIGHEST MEN'S TRIPLICATE (TEAM)

The record for the highest men's triplicate was set by the Stroh's Bohemian Beer team in Detroit, in 1950. Their combined score for each game in their three-game series was 1,144—a 229 average.

HIGHEST WOMEN'S TRIPLICATE (TEAM)

The highest women's team triplicate was bowled in May 1998 by Dianna Wilson, Joli Sutter, Maggie Blecha, Terri Foote, and Linda Cantwell while bowling in the T-Bird Ladies League at Thunderbowl in Wichita, Kansas. The team's combined score for each game in its three-game series was 856. The previous ladies' record, an 848 triplicate for a five-lady team, was set during the 1984–85 season by the H. R. Crabb and Son team in Arcade, New York.

MONEYMAKING MILESTONE

Left-handed great Earl Anthony was the first pro bowler to earn more than $100,000 in a year when he accomplished that feat in 1975. Anthony broke the million mark for career earnings in 1982.

YOUNGEST PBA TOURNAMENT WINNER

Phenom Norm Duke was only eighteen years old when he won the Cleveland Open in Cleveland, Ohio, making him the youngest bowler to take home the trophy at a PBA Tour event.

FIRST FULL SCHOLARSHIP

In November of 1997, Jennifer Daugherty became the first U.S. student to receive a full bowling scholarship to college. The scholarship came from the University of Nebraska, which Daugherty currently attends.

GLOSSARY

action	Pins knocking over pins, flying and mixing, ending with a strike or a good makable leave; also wagers made upon the outcome of matches.
address	Derived from golf. To address the alley (Helloooooo, alley!). To assume your stance at the start of your delivery; to set up.
alignment	Direction of your arm's arc of motion when it's the same direction as your target.
alley	The playing field, baby. Considered just a tad vulgar these days, like calling ladies "gals." The vogue term is *lane*.
anchor	The last bowler in the lineup of a team. Caboose.
angle of attack	The angle at which the ball hits the pins. The bigger the hook and the more sideways movement the ball has at impact, the greater the angle of attack.
baby split	Any split in which the pins are close enough together for a ball between them to knock down both.
backswing	A spare or strike in which the front pin falls last.
backdoor	The portion of the swing from the bottom of the downswing to the highest point behind the bowler. The higher the backswing, the faster the ball will be moving at the point of release.

backup	A ball that curves or "fades away" to the right (for a right-hander). In other words, the opposite direction of a normal hook.
bagger	Consecutive strikes. ("He's working on a three-bagger.")
balance arm	The arm that isn't rolling the ball. You should be working that wing like a tightrope walker, because it 's your key to balance.
ball rack	The portion of the ball run, alongside the approach, on which balls remain after their return from the pit. (The ball rack is now generally in the center of each pair of lanes.)
ball run	The tunnel underneath and between the lanes through which the ball is returned from the pit to the ball rack.
ball track	The portion of the lane worn from frequent use. It can be useful to those who naturally throw the ball along the groove's path, or a detriment to those who want to take a different path to the target.
break	Pins downed by the first ball.
British smile	A leave that resembles a dentist's nightmare.
Brooklyn side	The left side of the lane. A strike that hits on the "wrong" side of the headpin, a crossover strike, is said to hit on the Brooklyn side. A traditional pocket hit, therefore, occurs on the Jersey side.
channel	Those ditches-of-no-return on either side of the lane. A very polite word. Why has *trough* never caught on? Chances are when you're in it, you call it "a blankety-blank gutter!"

chop	Missing a spare by knocking down only one of two pins next to each other.
clip	Stop short on your backswing.
convert	Make a spare.
cover	Make a spare.
C.O.R.	Coefficient of restitution, or the amount of energy transferred from the ball to the pins at contact. The higher your ball's C.O.R., the more hitting power it has.
dancer	Pin bouncing end to end, or end over end.
delivery	Method with which you get from your stance to your release of the ball.
downswing	The portion of the swing that releases the energy, from the top of the backswing to the lowest point just before the release.
dump	To drop the ball early in your delivery; release the fingers from the ball too soon.
error	To mess up royally. An open frame, some-what less than ten pins felled with both balls.
fast feet	Feet moving too fast, so that they're out of sync with the swing of the ball during your delivery. You get there before the ball does and bad things happen.
fast lane	A lane, usually freshly oiled, that won't allow hooks to hook as much as they should.
finish	The final portion of your delivery as your slide foot slides and your fingers release the ball out onto the lane.
following the ball down	Getting leverage by bending forward at the waist during the opening steps of your delivery, so that your head and the bowling ball are both lowering at the same time.

foul	Stepping over the foul line or touching the lane beyond the line with any part of your body.
foul line	Line behind which a bowler must remain to legally deliver the ball. To touch beyond the line is to foul. Crossing this line is not just against everything bowling stands for but it's dangerous, too.
frame	One two-ball turn. The tenth and final frame has one or two bonus balls available, one for a spare and two for a strike.
full hit	Striking the target pin at or near the center.
full-roller	A ball that rolls along its equator, touching the lane with its full circumference as it rolls. A full-roller will roll straight—not necessarily what you want in this game.
game	Ten completed frames.
gutter ball	A ball that goes into the channel, or gutter.
handicap	To adjust the score between players or teams to compensate for a mutually agreed upon and mathematically derived superiority.
headpin	Also the No. 1 pin. The guy in front. Unlike the other pins, to knock down the headpin, you almost always have to hit it with the ball.
high hit	A hit in which the center of the ball strikes a pin. A high hit on the first ball means hitting the headpin right in the center instead of in the strike pocket, often resulting in an ugly split.
hook	A ball that breaks sharply to the left (for a right-hander).

hooking lane	High-friction lane, low on oil, allowing a big hook to be thrown. Sometimes proprietors put red lights over these.
illegal pinfall	Any pin knocked down in an illegal manner, such as by a pinsetter, a ball bouncing off the rear cushion, or a ball that bounced in and out of a channel (yeah, right, like *that* happens).
inside	The side of the bowler and the lane opposite his or her bowling arm.
in there	A ball in either the left or right strike zone.
kickboard	Boards on the sides of the pins that allow the pins to bounce off to do further damage.
lane	More polite than *alley*.
lane condition	The amount of friction on the lane, depending on the amount of use since the last oiling, as well as on such factors as heat and humidity.
lane finish	The tough plastic coating put over the wood of lanes to protect the wood from wear and tear.
leadoff	The first bowler in the lineup of a team.
leave	What's left after your first ball. Knock down eight for a two-pin leave.
left field	The area left of the headpin; the Brooklyn side.
lift	To give the ball an extra-tight roll by lifting it with the fingertips at the moment of release. It is the lift that pro bowlers get with their strong fingers that makes their bowling ball sound like the Charge of the Light Brigade as it thunders down the alley.

loft	Throwing the ball out onto the lane rather than rolling it. Often caused by the bending of the thumb and its resulting late release. Loft the ball too far and you can be called for a foul.
mark	Make a strike or spare.
match	Game or series of games played to a conclusion between individual opponents or teams. In match play, it is the number of games won rather than the number of total points scored that determines the winner.
medal play	Tournament in which the total number of points scored, rather than the total number of games won, determines the winner.
negative axis pole	The pole of the rotating globe, uh, bowling ball, farthest from impact.
opening up	The backward movement of your bowling shoulder during delivery. For a right-handed bowler, this will make the ball go to the right of the target.
outside	The side of the lane or the pins that's on the same side as your bowling arm.
perfect game	Twelve consecutive strikes; a 300 game.
pincount	Number of pins knocked down.
pindeck	The area on which the pins are set.
pit	The area behind the pins, where the ball ends up.
pocket	The spaces between the headpin and the Two Pin to the left, and the Three Pin to the right. A pocket hit is necessary to have any chance of getting a strike.
positive axis pole	The end of the bowling ball's axis of rotation that's closest to the target at impact.

pushaway	The start of the delivery. The ball moves horizontally from its position during the stance, to the start of the backswing.
rack	A full set of ten pins, freshly spotted and blissful in their ignorance; or the area on which those pins are set.
range finders	The dots and arrows on the track, there to help you line up your shot.
raw score	The actual score, a bowler's score before the handicap points are added.
release	The final part of the delivery, the actual moment that the ball comes off your fingertips.
reverse hook	Backup ball.
runway	The approach area, usually one step up from the score table.
scotch doubles	A two-on-two competition. One team member rolls the first ball; the other throws the second.
scratch	Using actual score, without handicaps.
series	Several games played together in a row by an individual bowler or teams. Most commonly, three.
setup	Stance.
sidewall	The high division boards between lanes at the deck end.
slow lane	Dry, high-friction lane, good for your hook.
span	The distance from your bowling ball's thumbhole to its finger holes.
spare	To use both balls to knock down all the pins in a frame. You knew that already, didn't you?

split	A leave that involves pins, alone or in groups, that are separated from one another. To roll your second ball through the middle without hitting pins on either side is sometimes called "kicking a field goal."
spot	A place on the lane where a bowler is aiming.
steal	To get more pins than you deserve by the hit made.
strick	To knock down all ten pins with the first ball. Boom; *X*.
strike zone	Target area on either side of the headpin.
supporting fingers	The fingers on your bowling hand that have no hole to go into. Hook 'em horns.
sweep	The device on the pinsetter that clears the plate.
sweepstakes	Tournament in which contestants pay an entry fee (for prizes).
target pin	The pin that must be hit to make a shot.
thin (hit)	Where the ball barely touches the pin—leading to chops, wobbles, and heartache.
three-quarter hit	First ball hits between the Two Pin and the Four Pin; or between the Three Pin and the Six Pin.
triplicate	Three games of identical scores bowled as a series by an individual or, cumulatively, by a team.
washout	An ugly leave in which the headpin as well as an assortment of others are left standing.
wobble	A pin that does the shimmy yet remains erect.

ABOUT THE AUTHOR

Michael Benson, who lives on the Brooklyn side with his wife and their two children, is the author of thirteen books.

INDEX

Golden Greek's Tavern and
  Bowling Lanes, 1–2
grip, 54
Guenther, John, 79
gutters, 2, 6, 7

half-bowls, 60
headpin, 3, 6, 8, 23
  spares and, 30
  "too much headpin," 27
heathen, 59
Henry VIII, king of England, 61
high hit, 34
holes, drilling, 53–55
Holland, bowling in, 60
hooks, 21, 23–26, 24–25, 27
  polyester balls and, 49
  Ten Pin leave and, 32
Hoskins, Steve, 78, 79

Illiano, John, 54
inside line shot, 24, 25
Irving, Washington, 62
Isemann, George, 70

Jaros, Steve, xii, 78
Johnston, Johnny, 65

Kasimakis, Rudy "Revs," xi–xiv,
  xiii, 18, 67
kegling, 60
Kressin, Myrt, 80

lane dressing, 44, 50
lanes, 2, 5, 6, 7
  Brooklyn Side of, 30
  oiliness of, 2, 16, 44, 49
LaRocco, Josey, 79
lawn bowling, 60
league nights, 3

leagues, 3, 64
Learn, Bob, Jr., 79
leaves
  defined, 29
  Seven Pin as, 32
  splits, 33–35
  Ten Pin as, 31–32
left-handed bowlers, 19, 21, 36,
  80
  shoes and, 56
  Ten Pin leave and, 32
lob, 73
Long Island Open, 66

Make That Spare (TV show), 65
marks, counting, 40
Mazza, John, 67
McCordic, Pete, 79
men, bowling and, 48, 80
midline ball setup, 11
Mineralite Ball, 63
miss, 3, 45
Monsey, John J., 72
Moore, C.K., 79
Mosayebi, Mark "Wasabi," 67
muscling the ball, 16–17

National Bowling Champions
  (TV show), 65
National Duckpin Bowling
  Congress (NDBC), 70–71
New York City Bowling
  Experience, 66
nine-pin break, 39, 42
ninepins, 60, 61, 62
Norris, Joe, 80

Ockerman, Troy, 77
Olympics, bowling in, 66
One Pin, 8, 21, 70